Unless By Invitation

Crimes That Shocked Ireland

Cróna Esler

BLACKWATER PRESS

ISBN 978-1-909974-00-5

BWP Ltd., 1-5 North Frederick Street, Dublin 1
Printed in the Republic of Ireland.
jloconnor@eircom.net

Acknowledgements

We often hear it said that there's at least one book in everyone and for the last number of years I have toyed with the idea of writing this exact book. Life sometimes gets in the way but for me, this idea kept knocking at my door. In late 2013, I began to take it seriously and as 2014 dawned, I made a promise to myself that *Unless By Invitation* would be in bookstores across the country by October.

Firstly, I wish to thank John O'Connor at Blackwater Press for believing in me and enabling me to realise my dream. Thanks also to Paula Byrne at Blackwater Press who designed the book.

To the serving and retired members of An Garda Síochána who assisted me with my research – particularly retired Superintendent Padraic O'Toole, retired Detective John Clancy, retired Garda Jim O'Keefe and retired Detective Basil Johnson – thank you.

I also want to acknowledge Padraic Nally, Sally Sweeney and Winnie McDonagh for taking time out to meet with me. Thanks too to Auriole and Marilyn Fountaine and to Tony Martin for facilitating my visit to Norfolk.

A word of thanks to the photographers who supplied pictures for the book – Henry Wills/*Western People*, Peter Wilcock, Ray Ryan/*Tuam Herald*, Courtpix, James Flynn/APX and *Eastern Daily Express*. Thanks also to Cormac Hanley in Claremorris who supplied a photo of his late uncle, Henry Dixon.

The search for photographs was often difficult and I wish to acknowledge the assistance of Mairead O'Shea in the *Roscommon Herald*, David Burke at the *Tuam Herald*, Dave O'Connell at the *Connacht Tribune*, Patsy Glynn, Gerard O'Loughlin and Margaret Cleary.

Thank you to two great friends and colleagues, *Western People* editor James Laffey and John Fogarty of *The Examiner*, for your advice and guidance along the way.

To my dear friends who continued to encourage me to write this book – and didn't complain when I disappeared for months – I say a huge thank you. It is several years since I first began to talk about the idea – to those who kept telling me it was a good idea, my sincere gratitude to you all for your belief in me.

To my parents, Bob and Mary, my brothers Cathal, Shane and Rory and my sister Derbhla, my heartfelt thanks for the late-night calls, all your encouragement and patience and for your advice and support every step of the way. Thanks to my mother-in-law Colette; to my sisters-in-law Louise, Olive and Elaine; and to my brothers-in-law Gary and Seán for your encouragement.

Finally, thank you to my husband Mike for always believing in me and for your moral support and understanding over the last number of months.

Cróna Esler
October 2014

Contents

- "For a man's house is his castle, et domus sua cuique est tutissimum refugium [and each man's home is his safest refuge]."

Introduction

There is nothing more sacred than a person's home. The home is where we raise our children; where we spend time in the intimate company of family and friends; where we return at the end of a day to rest; and where we live our private lives in peace. Our home is our shelter from the world and our place of security and refuge.

The Irish Constitution (Article 40.5) states that the dwelling of every person is inviolable and shall not be forcibly entered, save in accordance with the law. It echoes the old English proverb, "a man's home is his castle", which has been a legal precept in England since at least the 17th century – no one may enter another person's home, unless by invitation.

This was established as common law by the lawyer and politician Sir Edward Coke, in The Institutes of the Laws of England, 1628: "For a man's house is his castle, et domus sua cuique est tutissimum refugium [and each man's home is his safest refuge]."

Burglaries and thefts, unfortunately, are by no means a new phenomenon in society and in fact date back to the beginning of time. However, the early 1980s saw the dawning of a new era in rural Ireland when a new level of full-on violent confrontation was adopted by gangs and individuals.

Instead of homes being burgled in sneak attacks when people were at bingo or attending Mass, criminals began to set their sights on elderly and vulnerable people, mainly targeting those who were living alone in isolated areas. Bachelors, spinsters, widows and widowers were seen as easy targets and in many cases, kept large quantities of cash in their homes – stored under mattresses and in jars and biscuit tins.

Random attacks for gain on elderly and vulnerable people have become all too common across rural Ireland and the lengths to which people are permitted to go in order to protect their homes, their lives and their properties, has long been a talking point in Ireland.

In 2004, Padraic Nally became a household name all across Ireland when he shot and killed a Traveller on his farm in Co Mayo. But while Padraic Nally is often the name cited in the media, his was by no means an isolated case.

The vicious attacks on Mary Connell in Caherlistrane in Co Galway and on Edward and Peter Gilmore in Thomastown, Kilmaine in Co Mayo in December 1981 are examined in this book (Chapter 5). One of the brothers died at the scene that night and sadly, by the time the four perpetrators were brought to justice, all three of their victims were dead.

That very same year, 17-year-old Thomas Murray brutally murdered Willie Mannion in Ballygar in Co Galway and 19 years later, while on temporary release from prison, he struck again, killing his former teacher Nancy Nolan. These cases are also covered (Chapter 9).

87-year-old Margaret Glynn perished in a house fire at her home in Ahascragh in Co Galway in 1981 but while her death initially seemed like a tragic accident, Michael Kelly was later convicted of her murder. He continues to protest his innocence.

The village of Ahascragh was shook once again in 1993, when 59-year-old Bridget Glynn was found dead in her bed. Ironically, Ms Glynn's move to Ahascragh a few years earlier from the family holding at Eskermore was prompted by her growing fear of isolation. Willie Boden was convicted of her murder. Chapter 11 looks at the murders in Ahascragh.

In 1995, Mayo GAA legend Henry Dixon was targeted twice by thieves at his public house in Claremorris in Co Mayo. In the second incident, he was tied to his bed and badly beaten. The former football star never fully recovered from his attack and died in 1998.

Around the same time in Co Roscommon, gardaí were experiencing similar problems, with elderly people in isolated areas being targeted in their homes. The cases of Catherine Dillon and Christy Doyle were two such instances and in January 1998, Aidan Fallon was convicted of robbing and falsely imprisoning his two victims. These cases are dealt with in Chapter 7.

Pensioner Christy Hanley was robbed, beaten and left for dead in Kilbeggan, Co Westmeath in 2008. An estimated €10,000 was stolen from his home and Christy was found dead in his small cottage. Noel Cawley was later convicted of manslaughter and robbery (Chapter 15).

Of course, in October 2004, the shooting of a Traveller on a farm in Co Mayo sparked national debate about the rights of a homeowner and the right to defend one's property. The precarious legal position that existed in Ireland in relation to the protection of a person's home, their family and their property, was at the forefront of people's minds all across the country.

Padraic Nally was initially jailed for six years in November 2005 for the manslaughter of John 'Frog' Ward at Nally's home in Funshinaugh, Cross in Co Mayo on October 14, 2004. In October 2006, his manslaughter conviction was quashed and a retrial ordered when the Court of Criminal Appeal ruled that the trial judge erred in his direction to the jury.

The grounds for appeal were as obvious as they were compelling and the decision of the Court of Criminal Appeal was entirely predictable. In December 2006, at the retrial in Dublin's Four Courts, Padraic Nally was found not guilty of the manslaughter of John Ward.

Now, 10 years after the shooting in Cross, this book approaches the story in terms of the juxtaposition of two lives – that of a 60-year-old bachelor farmer in rural Ireland who had never come to the attention of the gardaí; and that of a 42-year-old traveller with a string of previous convictions for larceny and violent assault, among others.

The book traces the lives of Padraic Nally and John Ward up to and including that fateful afternoon in October 2004, when the two came face-to-face on the Nally farm in Funshinaugh, Cross in Co Mayo.

It also covers Padraic Nally's murder trial in Mayo, his conviction and sentencing, his appeal and his retrial. The book examines the reaction from both the Nally and the Ward camps following the farmer's eventual acquittal at Dublin's Four Courts in December 2006.

John Ward's sisters look back on their brother's life and give their reaction to the legal proceedings, while Padraic Nally talks about what life was really like during his 11 months behind bars and how he has coped since returning to life on the farm in Mayo.

The case of Norfolk farmer Tony Martin, who shot and killed a 16-year-old intruder in his home in 1999, was talked about in the media both in Ireland and the UK around the time of the Padraic Nally case. In fact, there were many suggestions in the national media in Ireland that the Norfolk man had contacted Padraic Nally following his release from prison and invited him to come and stay with him in the UK until the media spotlight died down. In Chapter 13, Tony Martin tells his story.

Supporters of Tony Martin and Padraic Nally called for changes in the law – both in the UK and Ireland – following the two incidents in 1999 and 2004.

The origins of the so-called 'castle doctrine' in Ireland can be traced as far back as the 14th century, when it was established that a killing performed in defence of one's home or to repel a burglar was justified. Legally, however, the reality was somewhat different.

The introduction of the Criminal Law (Defence and the Dwelling) Act 2011 went some way in addressing the precarious legal position that existed in Ireland in relation to the protection of a person's home, their family and their property. Chapter 17 examines the legislation, while Chapter 19 looks at some of the measures taken by An Garda Síochána to tackle crime in rural Ireland.

Prior to the incident on his farm in Co Mayo in October 2004, Padraic Nally was living with a fear so great that it had taken over his every waking moment. He was afraid to leave his house but was afraid to be there too. In his statements to gardaí following the shooting, the bachelor farmer said he was convinced he would be found dead in his bed or alternatively, would be forced to take his own life, such was his level of fear. To this day, while he sympathises with John Ward's family who have lost a brother, a husband, a father, Padraic Nally insists that he did not go looking for trouble, trouble came looking for him.

In the UK, Tony Martin's situation is similar. Like Padraic Nally, the Norfolk farmer had no idea what the future held when he was faced with two intruders in his home. In 2000, while serving a life sentence for the murder of Fred Barras, a fellow prisoner made an interesting comment to the farmer and it is a sentiment that remains with him to this very day – it is better to be judged by twelve than to be carried by six. Some of the victims in this book were never given such an opportunity.

Chapter 1
A Shooting in Cross

The birds were still singing in the trees when the media descended on Padraic Nally's country cottage at Funshinaugh, Cross, Co Mayo on Thursday, October 14, 2004.

It was 5pm on the cutting autumnal evening by the time the journalists and camera crews arrived. In quiet country villages all across the land, farmers were out tending to their herds but Padraic Nally – a man known for his love of the land – was in custody at Castlebar Garda Station. Another man lay dead on his property and the glaring eye of the national media was focused firmly on South Mayo.

As news of a murder investigation swept through the rural country village of Funshinaugh, many gathered at the once-idyllic setting to see for themselves if the growing rumours carried any truth. Unfortunately, the stories were more than rumours and the once-peaceful community was shattered by tales of a shooting.

A story was circulating that, following an altercation at a local farmer's house shortly after 2pm that day, a 42-year-old Traveller was fatally shot. Locals were in fear for their own safety and were anxious to find out exactly what had happened.

Several members of An Garda Síochána from various stations throughout the region were at the scene and access to the farmer's house, less than a mile from the main Cross to Glencorrib Road, was restricted.

As various media bodies and family and friends of both parties gathered, investigating Gardaí at the scene were adamant that nobody would hinder their progress.

Standing at the head of the road, Gardaí monitored all movements and the mood was pensive on the cold October evening. The media huddled together as the cutting breeze became too much to take.

The family of the deceased, eager to continue down the road that had been blocked off by Gardaí, argued their case with the members of the police force who were in attendance. The Gardaí, simply following orders, were quick to put an end to the Travellers' plans and assured them that the Superintendent and the Inspector in charge of the case would talk to them as soon as possible.

However, when a camera crew from one of the three national television stations was given access to the scene, the argument between the Travellers and the Gardaí intensified and the dead man's family demanded they be allowed down to the farmhouse.

Eventually, Superintendent Padraic O'Toole and Inspector Tom Fitzmaurice greeted the waiting crowd, and as Superintendent O'Toole began to brief the media, Inspector Fitzmaurice took one member of the Travelling party to the scene in his car.

Naturally, the investigation – led by Claremorris Gardaí – was at a very early stage that evening and Gardaí were at pains to keep quiet as to exactly what had occurred at the farm.

It was 2.20pm on the afternoon of Thursday, October 14, 2004, when the Gardaí first became aware of the extraordinary events that had unfolded minutes earlier in Funshinaugh. Garda Pauline Golden from Claremorris Garda Station received a phone call from Padraic Nally. He gave his name and address and told her that two fellows had come into his yard and he was afraid of them. Mr Nally claimed the men had been at his house the previous Christmas and he went on to explain that, a short time before making the call, he had taken out his gun and had shot one of the men. The farmer thought the man was dead; he was lying on the ground and had not moved.

On the phone to Garda Golden, Mr Nally sounded agitated and was out of breath at times. He gave the Garda directions to his house and Garda Golden contacted Sergeant James Carroll in Ballinrobe, before calling Inspector Tom Fitzmaurice and Sergeant Murray. Some minutes later, she received a call from Ambulance Control in Castlebar about the incident. At 2.40pm, she contacted Dr Regan in Cong and asked him to attend the scene. Fr Colm Kilcoyne was also called and asked to travel to Funshinaugh.

At the same time as Padraic Nally was calling Claremorris Garda Station, Tom Ward – the son of the deceased – arrived at Headford Garda Station. Garda Peadar Brick was on duty. Tom was upset and told the Garda his father had been shot, pleading with Garda Brick to follow him to the scene.

Tom ran from the station door and climbed into a blue Open Kadett, before taking off in the direction of Cross. Garda Brick followed him for a little over six miles until Tom stopped his car outside a new house with a stone wall frontage. Tom walked back to the patrol car, telling the Garda he wasn't going any closer and pointing up the road towards Padraic Nally's house.

By then, Gardaí from Claremorris had responded to Mr Nally's call and had made their way to the scene. Sergeant Jimmy Carroll approached the patrol car from the opposite direction and asked Garda Brick to stay with Tom. When Garda Brick spoke to Tom, the 18-year-old said he was afraid to go any closer to Nally's house and asked if he could sit in the back of the patrol car. He told Garda Brick that he and his father had pulled in at Nally's house that afternoon.

"We saw a car outside and my father thought to ask if it was for sale. I waited outside in the car. I heard a shot. A man came out of the house and said to me 'Is that your father inside?' I said 'yes'.

The man said 'He's not coming out'. I drove then to Headford Garda Station," Tom told Garda Brick.

As time passed, Tom became anxious to see his father and asked the Garda to drive closer to the scene. Garda Brick obliged and drove the patrol car to a location approximately 20 yards from Nally's house. At this stage, the ambulance and doctor had arrived and Sergeant Carroll came to the patrol car to inform Tom that his father – a man known as John 'Frog' Ward – had been seriously injured by a gunshot wound and his body was lying in a field. Tom started to cry and enquired from Sergeant Carroll if his father was dead. Sergeant Carroll nodded his head and put his hand on Tom's shoulder in sympathy.

When Tom realised the severity of the situation, he demanded to see his father's body.

"How did my father get there in the field? He was shot in the house the other side of the road," he told Gardaí. Tom got out of the patrol car and attempted to enter the field to walk over to where his father's body lay, but Garda Brick stopped him.

"I told him I wasn't arresting him but he couldn't go any further. The area was sealed off and no one could enter without authority," Garda Brick explained.

When Tom saw Padraic Nally however, his blood boiled.

"Are you going to arrest him for what he did to my father?" Tom asked.

"I suppose he'll get away with it, like always."

Tom got back into the patrol car and rolled the window down. Garda Brick told him he didn't know the position in relation to the investigation and said the facts would have to be established before anything could be done.

Tom was, understandably, incredibly upset at the scene. He expressed anger towards Padraic Nally, pointing him out to Gardaí.

"That is the man that shot my dad. If you don't do something, I will do it for ye," he warned.

Back in the patrol car, Garda Brick asked Tom what had happened that afternoon on Nally's farm.

"Me and my father stopped outside the man's house and my father went in enquiring about the sale of a white car. I waited outside. I heard a shot. I panicked. I revved the car. I saw a man come out of the house and he got into his white car. This man did not speak to me at any stage. I then drove to Headford," he responded.

Tom told Garda Brick that he wanted to ring his mother but he was unable to do so because the battery on his phone was dead. Garda Brick handed Tom his mobile phone but told him he shouldn't ring his mother with such devastating news.

"I explained that I could get the Gardaí in Galway to call to see her. Tom was upset. I opened the back door of the patrol car and stood beside him. Tom vomited on the road and then asked if he could go home. I told him I'd drop him home but he'd have to wait for the go-ahead from Inspector Fitzmaurice. I contacted Galway Garda Station to have Mrs Ward informed of the death and left word that her son could be contacted at Westport Garda Station."

***

As it happened, Superintendent Padraic O'Toole, who headed up the investigation, was off duty and away on leave when the shooting occurred.

"I got a phone call on the afternoon of October 14, and as soon as possible, I made my way to Cross. The Gardaí had been on the scene for some time and Padraic Nally was in the process of making a statement when I arrived," the retired superintendent recalled.

"Initially the scene was preserved, so I didn't enter the actual scene at that stage. The Inspector had been on duty and he was on the scene ahead of me so he updated me on the situation. At that stage, we were simply trying to establish the facts and not listen to rumours about what went on. If somebody, at a scene like that, tells you something happened, then you need to establish what evidence that is based upon. You're trying to establish the facts," he explained.

At that stage, the Gardaí were unsure of what exactly had occurred on the farmyard of Padraic Nally.

"We hadn't fully established the circumstances. We knew there had been a shooting. We knew a person was dead. We knew there was another person arrested and taken away – that was John Ward's son. We were trying to put the pieces together and see what fitted and what didn't, based on the evidence we had," he added.

When Superintendent O'Toole arrived in Funshinaugh, the scene had already been blocked off to pedestrians and traffic. Nobody was allowed near Padraic Nally's farmyard, apart from the investigating Gardaí.

"We were trying to deal with a shooting and a death but we had to look at all sides of the story," he said.

While the Gardaí were busy dealing with a crime scene, Superintendent O'Toole was conscious that there was a family grieving too. "There were family members of the dead man who were anxious to get to the scene and I allowed them access to see John's body. We were unable to allow them into the field where his body lay so they remained on the roadway. By then, there was a crime scene tent over the body and we were waiting for the State Pathologist to arrive."

"When something like this happens, you have to try to take everyone's concerns and feelings into consideration. We understood that there were a lot of people affected by the incident – Padraic Nally and John Ward and their extended families and also the local and the Travelling communities. From a humanitarian point of view, we had to allow some members of the family to go up and see where the body lay. We couldn't allow them into the field because it would contaminate the whole scene and hinder the investigation as a result. Of course, that was difficult too – we were dealing with a grieving family but they couldn't be allowed into the field to where the body of their loved one lay," he remembered.

Despite the sensitivity of the scene, Superintendent O'Toole also recognised the media interest in the situation.

"There was huge interest locally, nationally and internationally and we were conscious of that too. We allowed one television camera crew and one photographer up to the scene to get their footage, on the condition that it would be shared with the other media outlets. I suppose, regardless of what we were doing, it was important for us to try to understand that the media needed footage for the evening news, and even though we were in the middle of an investigation, we had to appreciate that too. We were aware that broadcasts had to go out, while the print media wasn't quite as urgent. We allowed cameras access, knowing that, once they got what they wanted, they'd be out of our hair for a while," he explained.

Making sure all angles were covered, Superintendent O'Toole only allowed cameras to the scene on the agreement that whatever footage was shot and whatever pictures were taken, would be shared among all media outlets present. "We let them nominate who would go to the scene, on the agreement they would circulate photos and camera footage to the others. We had to control the situation, we couldn't have every single media outlet up around the scene; we had a serious job on our hands."

In the weeks and months prior to the death of John Ward, Padraic Nally had been unable to sleep properly at night and was constantly rushing home from the mart or from his herding, fearful that his house would be targeted by thieves.

Following a break-in at his home the previous February, he had moved his gun to the shed by the house and had placed it in a barrel with a bag covering the weapon. The cartridges, he kept in a bucket beside the barrel. His gun was always loaded.

"I had one bullet in the gun at all times. The bullets were three or four years old because I hadn't been doing much shooting," he said.

The single barrel shotgun that the farmer owned was approximately 65 years old.

"It was my father's gun and after he died I decided to keep the gun and put the licence in my name. I wasn't doing much with it. It was only ever used for shooting magpies or crows," Padraic recalled.

On the afternoon of October 14, 2004, Padraic Nally was out in one of his fields erecting a fence. At 1.30pm, he came in for his dinner and after eating, he sat and listened to the radio. He had just heard a few news headlines on Galway Bay FM when he was distracted by a revving noise outside.

"A car was being revved to the last so I went out the front door, out the gate and across to the car in the laneway. The driver called me over and asked me how much I wanted for my car. He was trying to attract my attention and I smelled a rat.

'Where's your mate?' I said to him.

He told me he was gone to knock at the back door; he didn't tell me it was his father," said Mr Nally.

When the farmer went to the back of his house, he saw John Ward crouching down and pushing in his back door. Mr Nally turned and went to the shed for his gun, only intending to give John Ward a warning.

"I got my gun for protection – there were two of them and only one of me."

Nally claimed that when he emerged from the shed, John Ward was in his kitchen. He moved towards the back door from the shed and John Ward ran out.

"The gun went off accidentally in my hand, I didn't fire at him. I was holding it down at my hip. I remember my hand shaking. The fear was in me that I was going to be killed at that particular stage. When I fired the shot, I thought he'd run, but he didn't," he said.

Nally claimed Ward then ran towards him and caught his throat, before the farmer pushed him to the ground on a green patch.

"I held him down. He tried to kick me in the stomach and in the balls. He had his two shoes against my stomach at one stage; he was very strong and I had an awful job to hold him down," Padraic explained.

Mr Nally said John Ward then caught him by the right wrist and he found it difficult to free himself. "He grabbed my gun and rose it up to hit me on the left side but I caught hold of the gun and took it from him. He stood up and went for me again."

Padraic Nally's evidence in court was that he then left the gun down and caught the intruder by the throat, swinging him back against the door. John Ward tried to kick and push the farmer. "It all happened so fast. I was in a state and thought the other lad [Tom] would come. He [John] kept calling 'Tom, Tom'," he said.

Mr Nally then pushed Mr Ward onto his back, picked up a stick and began hitting him.

"I hit him on the head, hands and feet. I must have hit him 20 times. I did it to save myself, I was afraid," Mr Nally explained.

According to the farmer, when John Ward got up again, he pushed him back into a pile of nettles.

"I made for the gun and for the shed to get more cartridges. I was afraid more of them would come and try to kill me," he added.

Nally said he remembered looking out and seeing John Ward running out the gate. He reloaded the gun and brought two extra cartridges with him. Nally ran out to the road and fired a shot. Ward fell to the ground and Nally knew he was dead.

The Mayo farmer then lifted John Ward into the field because he didn't want anyone to see the body on the road.

"If that fella in the car came back with more people and saw the body, they would have killed me straight away. I didn't know what I was doing, I was going to shoot myself after that," Nally explained.

In the week before the shooting at his farmyard in Funshinaugh, Mr Nally had been thinking about taking his own life. He later admitted that if John Ward had escaped uninjured that day, he would have killed himself rather than go through it all again.

Tom Ward, who was driving the car on October 14, 2004, had quite a different telling of the incident on Padraic Nally's farm.

He and his father got up at the usual time that morning and his father – John 'Frog' Ward – suggested they go for a spin because he was looking to buy a car. Tom was driving an Open Kadett which, he said, he had purchased the day before. He told Gardaí he paid €180 for the car on the outskirts of Galway City but would not say who sold him the vehicle.

After 1pm that day, he stopped the car outside a shop on the Galway side of Headford. Tom bought a bottle of Smirnoff and a box of Benson & Hedges cigarettes. He drove on into Headford and out the Cross Road. When he came to a junction, his father told him to turn left. Tom claimed he did not know where he was going. "We drove on a road for a mile or two and came to a T-junction and my father told me to turn right. I drove down the road and my father told me to stop at a house. I drove into the yard and he had a chat with the man. This man worked with headstones. My father gave him his mobile number for some reason," he said.

Later, during the trial into the death of John Ward, Tom admitted his father never possessed a mobile phone.

After a few minutes talking to this man, John Ward got back into the car and instructed his son to drive down the road and turn right.

"We drove for a hundred yards before my father told me to stop outside a house. He got out and went into the house to see if the van was for sale. It was an Opel van. He went to the side of the house and had a look at the van. He knocked at the front door. There was nobody there so he came back out and we moved on."

The next stop for John and Tom Ward was at the home of Padraic Nally in Funshinaugh, Cross in Co Mayo. It was a decision Tom lived to regret.

"I drove until we saw a white car parked on the right-hand side of the road at the side of a house. 'Turn here, that car could be bought,' my father said.

I turned the car and went back to the house and then reversed in beside the car, leaving the engine running. My father got out of the car and walked in the gate, just behind where the white car was parked – a white Nissan. I was sitting in the car, looking over my left shoulder as my father went into the house."

It was at this moment that Padraic Nally approached Tom.

"A man came out of the house and spoke to me.

'What do you want?' he asked.

I asked him if the car was for sale and told him we were interested in buying it.

'Who is inside there?' he asked.

I told him my father was looking for the owner of the car. From the tone of his voice, he seemed to be annoyed.

'Is he? He won't be coming out of it', he said and then he walked to the shed," Tom recalled.

"I kept looking and the next time I saw him, he was coming from the shed and heading for the house. He was carrying a shotgun. He had it pointed; held in both hands down at his chest. As he walked on towards the house I lost sight of him. The next thing I heard was a bang from the gun. I heard my father moaning. I got frightened and drove onto the road. I turned right and stopped down the road a few yards to see if my father would come out. I looked over my left shoulder and saw the man in the middle of the road, facing me. He walked back in and he reversed out the white car and went in the opposite direction. I drove off, I was afraid."

According to Tom, he then drove to the main road. He stopped a blue car and asked the occupants to ring the Gardaí. They said they had no phone.

He continued towards Headford and came to Glencorrib where there was a van parked, facing towards Cross. Again, Tom stopped the car and asked the driver to ring the Gardaí. He too said he had no phone.

Tom stopped a third vehicle and conveyed the same message. The driver said he would ring the Gardaí but was in a hurry and drove off.

Tom drove towards Headford and asked a pedestrian for directions to the Garda station. It was here he met Garda Peadar Brick, who followed him back to the scene.

Tom claimed he had never been in the Funshinaugh area prior to that day. As far as he was aware, his father had never been in the area either.

Tom told Gardaí that immediately after he heard a shot being fired at the rear of Padraic Nally's house, he drove out onto the road.

"I turned right as far as a house on the left-hand side. I pulled in there and stopped for a minute or two. I turned then at that house and drove up past the farmer's house again. I was looking into the yard but I couldn't see anybody. I drove up the road again and turned outside a house on the left and then came back down again. As I drove past I was calling my father. I shouted 'Daddy, Daddy' a few times but I saw nobody. I was too afraid to go in. I stopped outside for a minute and then moved on.

I turned again outside a house and drove up past the farmer's house again and went further up the road. I went around the bend and then turned outside another house. I think I was stopped outside that house for a few minutes. I was trying to decide what to do. I drove down past the farmer's house again and stopped a short distance below the house but I didn't get out.

I looked back over my shoulder and saw the farmer walk out on the road. I drove down the road a bit further away from him and stopped. I saw the white car reverse out onto the road and drive off in the other direction. I couldn't see who was driving it. I reversed back to the entrance to the yard again and started calling to my father. I shouted a few times and then drove to the junction at the main road."

It was at this point that Tom decided to drive to Headford Garda Station.

***

Detective Garda Mick Conway, who met Padraic Nally at the scene in Funshinaugh that afternoon, said that one of the first things Nally said to him was that he was 'thinking of ending it'. Nally repeatedly told the Gardaí that he was 'out of his mind with worry'.

Detective Conway had arrived at the scene at 3.05pm and cordoned off the area. John 'Frog' Ward had been pronounced dead by Dr Michael Regan at 2.55pm. When Detective Conway spoke to the accused at the gate of his house, Nally told him: "I'm not feeling that well; I'm thinking of ending it altogether."

Nally told the detective that when he went around to the back of the house, he saw a man crouched down pushing in the back door. He went to the shed and got his gun and then went to the back door and shot the man. A struggle developed and after a while, he went back to the shed. When he saw the man running down the road, he shot him.

Detective Conway later arrested Tom Ward, the son of the deceased, on suspicion of burglary and brought him to Westport Garda Station. He was questioned under Section 4 of the Criminal Justice Act and was released without charge shortly after 10pm that night. Tom Ward did not accept he was there to burgle the house.

Padraic Nally was also arrested that evening. He was taken to Castlebar Garda Station and questioned under Section 30 of the Offences Against the State Act.

In the course of the interview, Mr Nally said he had seen Tom Ward at his house before that day. It was the previous summer and Tom had stopped to ask for directions to the lake.

"I can say with fair certainty that the young lad called to the house last May or June."

Later in the interview, Nally told Gardaí that when he asked Tom Ward where his mate was, he knew there was something wrong.

"Detective work is detective work. I smelled a rat. When I got up yesterday morning, I knew something was going to happen. I was expecting them back. When my sister left on Sunday evening, I cried. I said to her: 'There'll be changes when you're back'. I had a premonition. I had a good idea this was going to happen."

Nally went on to explain that when he saw the man crouching at the back door of his house, he recognised him from the Saturday fortnight before that when he was driving a black car and was looking for directions to the lake to go fishing.

On October 14, 2004, he asked John Ward: "What are you doing in there, you rogue?" He then went to the shed to get his gun.

Nally stated that when he shot Ward, the victim went straight for him but the farmer knocked him to the ground. There was a struggle and they exchanged a few blows. The victim was trying to catch him by the collar and pull him down and tried to 'kick [him] in the balls'.

Nally said John Ward grabbed the gun and tried to hit him with it. He went for Ward by the throat and pushed him against the jamb of the back door. "It was a real movie-type effort," Nally explained.

The farmer told Gardaí that he got an ash stick and beat John Ward about the head. He had struck Ward on the head, hands and feet about 20 times altogether. When Ward started calling for his son, Nally was concerned about the other man in the car.

He pushed John Ward and knocked him on the flat of his back on top of a heap of nettles. He then returned to the shed to get cartridges to reload his gun, before following Ward to the road where he aimed and shot him.

"He was dead. There was no movement out of him. I put my hands under his arms and pulled him across the road and threw him across the wall," Nally said in the interview.

The 60-year-old farmer told Gardaí that Ward's head had not struck the wall. The injuries to the head were from the beating he gave him with the stick.

Nally went back to his house and closed the doors. He did not go near the back door as he wanted to 'leave it for evidence'. He then got into his van and went to Michael Varley's house.

Later, back at the house when the Gardaí arrived, he was feeling suicidal and 'was out of [his] mind with these people calling all the year'.

Nally said in his statement that the previous February his back door had been burst in and his chainsaw taken. He thought it must have been the same fellows. He was edgy about the second man as he thought he might go for him with an iron bar or a knife. He said that John Ward was 'well stunned' after the beating but he himself was 'out of [his] mind with worry' and he did not know what he was doing. At one stage Ward had him by the throat so he struck him with the stick.

"It was like hitting a stone or a badger. You could hit him but you could not kill him," Nally told Gardaí.

In his statement to Gardaí that night, Nally said he knew something like this was going to happen. He always expected it to happen on a Thursday. When he went to the shed to get his gun, he intended to fire a shot over Ward's head to frighten him but when he 'got him going into the house, [Nally] went berserk entirely'.

Superintendent O'Toole, who was in charge of the investigation into the shooting of John Ward at the Funshinaugh farmyard, had never come into contact with Padraic Nally prior to October 14, 2004.

To the ordinary person on the street, by the time Superintendent O'Toole arrived at the scene that day, the investigation was practically solved. But, for the Gardaí, it wasn't quite that simple.

"We had a statement from early on in the investigation, which meant we didn't have to look for someone unknown in relation to the shooting. Having said that, we still had to verify that what we were being told was supported by the other available evidence," explained the retired Superintendent.

"Our function was the same, no matter what we were dealing with. As Gardaí, we wanted to establish the facts and this investigation was treated no differently to any other. Sure, there was a huge amount of interest in the case nationally, but from a Garda point of view, the processes and procedures were the same as always," he stressed.

As the investigation into the death of John 'Frog' Ward began in earnest on the afternoon of October 14, 2004, the Gardaí were mindful that there were two families and two communities affected by the incidents that had occurred on the farm of Padraic Nally.

"Regardless of the rights and wrongs of what John Ward was or wasn't doing on the day and regardless of the rights and wrongs of what Padraic Nally did, there were still two families involved and everyone paid a heavy price. Clearly John Ward and Padraic Nally were at the centre of the events but there were the families, communities and neighbours involved too," explained the retired superintendent.

"All across rural Ireland, the fear of crime may not have been to the fore in the minds of ordinary people prior to the incident on Padraic Nally's farm, but it certainly was afterwards. The media were looking at this as a settled community versus Travelling community issue but from our point of view and from the point of view of the investigation, it didn't matter who was involved. There were a lot of life sentences, that's the reality.

Padraic Nally and the Ward family will have to live with the events of that fateful afternoon for the rest of their lives."

Chapter 2
Padraic Nally – Early Life

His was a simple life. Born and bred on the family farm in Funshinaugh, just outside the small rural village of Cross in Co Mayo, Padraic Nally's childhood was spent roaming his father's farm. Even as a boy, he had a special connection with nature and the animals. He would often spend his days wandering through the peaceful fields, looking for some twigs to build a treehouse or simply skipping through the land he knew so well.

Growing up away from the bright city lights and social scene that so many others of his age were enjoying, there was nowhere in the world Padraic would have rather been. He never craved a move to Galway or Dublin – or indeed further afield – he was content with his idyllic surroundings and with his own company.

Before Padraic was born, his father and mother had bought the farm in Funshinaugh and built the small cottage where he now lives. His father, Patrick, had grown up in the next village of Castletown. Padraic's mother, Mary, hailed from Tourmakeady, 25 miles north of Cross in Co Mayo. As a teenager, Patrick Nally had left his home in the west of Ireland in search of a better life in the United States but after a few years, he realised Ireland was the only place he could ever call home. When he returned home to Mayo and married Mary, they set up home in Funshinaugh.

Padraic was the couple's first born, arriving into the world on January 30, 1944. His sister, Maureen, was born the following year. The siblings were educated at Cross National School, making the two-mile journey by foot each day. After fourth class in Cross, Padraic left school. Maureen continued with her education, progressing to secondary school in Headford in Co Galway, just eight miles up the road. She later went on to teacher training college in England but Padraic had no such desire. He remained at home.

"I left school for good at 14-and-a-bit to help on the family farm. The work involved feeding the stock, milking the cows and working in the bog. I always wanted to live and work on the farm from an early age. Growing up, dad wasn't in good health for a long time so I had to do a lot of the work, but I didn't mind. This was land I was familiar with all my life. We kept cattle and sheep – it was mixed farming with a bit of tillage," Padraic explained.

Times were different then and life in Cross was very quiet.

"People hadn't much and nearly all the food was produced on the farm. The area has gotten more built up over the years and there are more houses now around the village. Those days, at the back end of the year, you'd have a couple of sheep and a couple of cattle for selling at the mart, that's all."

As a child, Padraic loved movies and he was just 10 when he first experienced the pictures. "I went to see my first film in a marquee across the fields. They used to have the pictures in marquees that time and it was like stepping into a whole other world," he recalled.

In his teenage years and into his twenties, Padraic continued to go to the pictures in Ballinrobe or Kilmaine and sometimes at Cong's Ashford Castle, which is just eight miles from his home.

"In Ashford, there used to be pictures shown regularly but you mightn't be let in some nights at all. They had spaces there for tourists and a certain number of locals would be let in too. Then if there was high gentry staying at Ashford, it'd be a closed shop that night."

There were dances at the time in Cong Dance Hall and crowds rolled in from all over to attend. But the dances weren't really Padraic's cup of tea. "I was more interested in going to the pictures than in dancing," he admitted.

Of course, Padraic has remained a bachelor all his life and the truth is he never really thought about marrying. "It wasn't really something I ever considered. I was helping out here at home on the farm and then I got too old for moving out. Maureen never married either. She lives between Knockmore and Foxford in North Mayo. Maureen went from school straight to college in England and when she was finished with her studies, she got a teaching post in Ballina so she never moved back here again. We're still very close though and she comes home to Funshinaugh every weekend," he explained.

In his twenties, Padraic joined the Civil Defence, Macra na Feirme and the Irish Farmers' Association (IFA).

"I joined the Civil Defence in 1964 and I spent about 25 years in it. We were doing a rescue in Cong at the time of the Nuclear Fallout. We'd be scaling ourselves down off the side of a mountain on ropes, making chair ropes and tying knots; we were at it for about two months. Then when the Foot and Mouth scare came about, it was called off," he said.

Padraic enjoyed his time in the Civil Defence. "It was like a pastime for the winter. We'd go to the meetings. We were in Knock for the Pope's visit and we were down there for two days for the opening of Knock Airport. I really enjoyed it. We had thought of doing fire drills and having a fire-shed in Cong but that was knocked on the head because there was no building available for it. I joined Macra then for a few years," he added.

Over the years, Padraic also took part in IFA protest marches in various parts of the country, including Dublin and Kerry.

By the age of 27, he had acquired a tractor and a car – the first motor vehicle in his home, as neither of his parents were able to drive. However, he never owned a telephone until his sister purchased a mobile phone for him, following the incident at his farm in October 2004.

Padraic's father passed away in 1991, leaving just him and his mother at home in Funshinaugh. "My mother did the housework and she used to have hens and pigs and she'd help with the farm and the cows as much as she could too. I was out on the farm, seeing to the animals and the land. My mother passed away in 1999 and it has just been me here by myself ever since, apart from at weekends when Maureen comes to stay."

As the years passed, Padraic began to become a regular at card games in Cross and the surrounding villages. Public houses had never really been his scene so the card games served to provide a social outlet for the placid farmer.

Padraic also regularly visited marts and agricultural shows in Ballinrobe, Maam Cross, Athenry and indeed throughout counties Mayo and Galway. It wouldn't be unusual for him to attend various marts and shows three or four times a week. However in 2001, things began to change and several incidents, both at his own house and at neighbours' houses, led the farmer to become extremely fearful for his safety.

"I had always enjoyed farming. I loved living in a rural area and spending time out on the land but in 2001, it started to get rough on me. People were calling and taking things out of my yard."

Padraic got so upset and concerned about the situation that he had taken to throwing water on clay around his gate any time he would leave the house, in order to see if there were any footprints in the clay when he returned home.

"I'd look for footprints or tyre tracks in the clay and often I'd find that people had been calling around while I was out."

He explained that in 2001, his house had been broken into and blankets and plates stolen. He reported this occurrence to the Gardaí in Ballinrobe.

In February 2004, intruders broke into his house via the back door and took a chainsaw that had been lying in the back bathroom of his bungalow farmhouse. On this occasion, Padraic had come home to find that his dressing table and that of his sister had been gone through. The dresser in the kitchen was ransacked too.

Padraic's shot gun had also been kicked under the bed in his room and it wasn't until almost two weeks later that he found the gun. "I thought it had been stolen but when I realised it was under the bed I knew it wasn't safe to leave it in the house any longer," he said.

The farmer didn't feel safe in the knowledge that whoever had been in his house now knew where he kept the weapon. "I was afraid that if I left my gun there, I'd be found dead in my bed some morning – shot by my own gun – so I decided to move it out to the shed," he added.

Following this incident, Padraic subsequently made a number of attempts to report the break-in and thefts to the Gardaí in Ballinrobe but when he called to the station on two separate occasions, there was nobody there to record his complaint.

Mr Nally also spoke of a separate incident that had left him shaken.

"One night at 2am I heard the dogs barking in the kitchen. I suspected that something was wrong so I got up and went to see what was happening. Somebody had lifted the latch of the back door. I was afraid and I rushed to the front door of the house, just in time to see a car driving away," he explained.

In August 2003, prior to the chainsaw being stolen from his home, a barrel had been taken from his yard and a number of vice grips and wrenches had been taken by strangers.

Following the shooting at Padraic Nally's farm in October 2004, locals described the then 60-year-old as 'an honest, quiet and hard-working farmer'. Nobody could have predicted the tragedy that would occur at Mr Nally's property, when 42-year-old John 'Frog' Ward was shot dead.

In the wake of the events on October 14, 2004, friends and neighbours rallied to help Mr Nally, offering 100% support to the farmer.

At the time, local Fine Gael Councillor Patsy O'Brien described Mr Nally as being very popular in the village and said Padraic was by no means a violent man.

"If you knew him you'd understand how much of a gentleman he is. He wouldn't harm a fly. What happened on the farm is beyond belief and the entire community is in a state of shock. For Padraic to shoot at someone, he obviously found himself in a situation where he was forced to act in such a manner. Unfortunately his whole life has changed as a result," he commented.

Chapter 3
John Ward – Early Life

John Ward was 42 years of age when he arrived on the farm of Padraic Nally in Funshinaugh, Cross in Co Mayo in October 2004. A man with upwards of 80 previous convictions, John's name had been notorious within criminal circles and he was known to Gardaí all across the country. His convictions dated back to November 1978, when he was found guilty of malicious damage at a sitting of Dundalk District Court.

Across almost three decades, John was convicted of crimes ranging from road traffic offences to larceny, from criminal damage to assault, from handling and receiving stolen goods to trespassing, and from drugs charges to public order offences.

At the time of his death, there were four bench warrants out for his arrest and there were a number of incidents throughout his life where the violence displayed by John Ward featured prominently in evidence when the matters came before various courts throughout Ireland.

On August 19, 1999, John entered a licenced premises on Main Street in Ballyshannon in a drunken state. When one of the barmen refused to serve him more alcohol, John threatened him with a Stanley knife. The barman later withdrew his complaint but nonetheless, Ward appeared before Ballyshannon District Court on March 15, 2000, where he was fined £200 for using threatening behaviour in a public place.

On April 30, 2000, Ward attacked a car at Market Yard in Sligo with a slash-hook, breaking the back window and side windows. There were two children and a woman in the car at the time of the incident. When he appeared before Ballyshannon District Court on June 15, 2001, to face charges in relation to the incident, he received a four-month prison sentence for possession of an article and a further three months in prison for assault. A second assault charge, as well as two charges under the Public Order Act, were taken into consideration by the judge.

On June 6, 2000, John Ward head-butted a prison officer at the Courthouse on Bridge Street in Donegal, while he was being removed from the local district court by prison officers. He subsequently appeared before Donegal District Court on January 3, 2001, and was sentenced to four months in prison for assault.

On April 25, 2002, a member of the Gardaí from Swinford Garda Station was investigating a crime at Sandyhill, Charlestown in Co Mayo, when he encountered John Ward. Ward produced a slash-hook and threatened the Garda. He was not made amenable for this incident because the investigating member was unable to effect service of summonses on him.

On May 15, 2004, Ward again produced a slash-hook and threatened members of the Gardaí at Carrowbrowne Halting Site on the Headford Road in Galway. He was arrested and charged with a number of offences, which included possession of an offensive weapon and being drunk and disorderly in a public place.

Despite John Ward's checkered background however, he was a loving son, brother, husband and father and even all these years later, John's family remember him as a smiling, carefree character – an important and much-loved member of the Ward family who was taken from them far too young.

John was the fourth born in a family of 15. His parents, John and Kathleen – or Kate as she was known – met and married in Ballaghaderreen. John Snr was a native of Leitrim, Kate was from Tipperary.

The family didn't have much when the children were growing up but they were happy. John was very close to his 14 siblings – Mary, Eileen, Kathleen, Tom, Christine, Charlie, Winnie, Gerard, Bridget, Jimmy, Nora, Josephine, Paddy-Joe and Sally. The seven eldest children were born in England, where John Snr and Kate had settled in their early years of marriage. The younger eight were born in Ireland.

Before eventually settling in Ballyshannon, the family lived between camp sites around Ballyshannon and Manorhamilton. John spent his early years in school in Manorhamilton and made his Communion there. The family were later given a house on the Station Road in Ballyshannon.

John's sister, Winnie McDonagh, was five years younger than John and has fond memories of her brother.

"We went from camp to camp as children. As a child, John loved school. He played football and other bits of sport. He had medals for soccer and he was always sporty. He got involved in any activities that were going on. We were a close family, we used to do everything together when we were young, whether that was shopping or playing outside, we'd all play together. If our father and mother were away, we'd all wait together at home. If John was the oldest in the house when my parents were away, he'd be the boss and whatever he said, went. There'd be no out or no town. He was in charge. We were poor growing up – we had nothing – but we were all good friends," she recalled.

When the family moved to Ballyshannon, they mixed well with the community there.

"We were well known to the settled people, they didn't class us as tinkers. We were well settled in with the community and they were for us," she added.

John Snr and Kate were strict on their children. "We always had to go to Mass on a Sunday. Let it snow or let it rain, you went to Mass. Confessions were on Saturdays and we went every two weeks. We went to bed at nine and even if we were allowed stay up a bit later, the television would be turned off. The adult films – or the wrong films as my father called them – would be on after nine and we wouldn't be allowed to watch them. Our parents were old-fashioned strict," Winnie explained.

When John left school, he got a job with local TD James White.

"He used to go to Lisdoonvarna with James to work in a hotel there. James White had a chicken factory as well and John and some of my other brothers used to work there too. At Christmas, they'd be plucking the turkeys and all that. He really enjoyed it. In his young life, he had a good life, he was happy," she said.

John Snr bought and sold scrap for a living. Sally, the youngest daughter, remembers going off into the countryside on the horse and cart with her dad. It was something all of the children did growing up and John learned the trade from his father.

"He was working in the hotels and the chicken factory in his early teens and he enjoyed that. My father used to go to different houses and ask for old cans or pots and John would often go with him on those journeys. My father used to do a bit of tinsmithing as well, putting bottoms in buckets and that sort of thing. He'd get scrap off people – heavy scrap or batteries or aluminium. He'd load it up into the cart and the boys would help him.

They'd sell it off then and get a few pound for it. John also did that for a lot of years himself and his son Tom used to go with him, just like he used to go with his father. They'd be gathering scrap and selling it and buying and selling old cars too. John and Tom might buy an old scrap car for €100 and then they might do it up or use a part and sell it off for €150 or €200," Winnie explained.

***

When John was 17, he married Marie McDonagh. It was an arranged marriage, like most of his other siblings. The newlyweds lived in the UK for a period before moving to Sligo. They went over and back to England for a number of years and lived between Donegal and Sligo whenever they were at home in Ireland. Eighteen months before his death, John and Marie moved to the Carrowbrowne Halting Site on the Headford Road in Galway.

According to his sisters, Winnie and Sally, John was a wonderful father to the couple's 11 children – Kathleen, Charlie, John Paul, Tom, Geraldine, Cindy, Caroline, Brian, Jason, Terry and Gerry.

"He was a very good father to his children. He would wash, cook and clean for them. If Marie sat down, she wouldn't have to get up again. John would go off for the day to make a living and then he'd stop on the way home and buy the food and bring it back and cook the dinner. He could put down a dinner better than I could put it down. He could fry a breakfast better than I could. Or to make a cup of tea was better than myself. He was very good to the kids, he really adored his family," Winnie explained.

Since the children were small, John was always a hands-on father.

"You could say he reared them up himself. When Marie would go into hospital to have the babies, you wouldn't have to mind his kids for him. John was there to change the nappies or comb the hair of the girleens. He'd feed them and look after them, he was a good father and they should never forget him," she added.

Winnie and John were close growing up and after Winnie and her husband – Bernard McDonagh – moved to Ballyhaunis, John would visit several times each week.

"He could knock on the door at six in the morning. I might be trying to sleep but John would call and he'd want the tea. He could also call at seven in the evening. He'd come to see me every second or third day; he used to visit me a lot when I was staying in Ballyhaunis," she said.

All of a sudden however, in September 2004, John stopped calling to see Winnie. What she didn't know however was that her brother had been admitted to hospital for psychiatric treatment. He had been hearing voices, experiencing hallucinations and was often depressed.

John was an in-patient in the Psychiatric Department at the University College Hospital in Galway from September 3 to 21, 2004. He was readmitted on October 1 as an emergency and remained in hospital until October 12. Two days later, he was dead.

"Before that, I'd see him every second or third day, he'd always come to visit. Then he stopped coming and I found it funny that he had stopped. I rang Marie a few times and asked her where he was. She'd tell me he was gone away and that she'd get him to ring me in the evening or the next day, but the call would never come. He was 'in the mental' but nobody knew. She was covering it all up," Winnie recalled.

Winnie wasn't the only one who was unaware of the situation. None of John's siblings were informed that he was in hospital. Interestingly, it wasn't John who was keeping his family in the dark. The decision was made by Marie.

"It wasn't that John was hiding it from his siblings and at a later time, Marie told me that John was wondering where we were and why we weren't contacting him or calling to see him. It was Marie's decision not to tell the family. Before he died, I hadn't seen him in a good few weeks," she continued.

John's sister Sally Sweeney was also unaware of her brother's stay in the Psychiatric Unit in Galway but towards the end of his second period in hospital, Sally got wind of the news and she went to visit him. "I was in to see him in Galway two or three days before he died. I had no idea he was in there before that and as soon as I heard it, I went to see him. We had a great chat, we talked about everything. There was no danger in him. He looked great and he was in great form. He even got the nurse to make me a cup of tea. He needed a haircut and he was telling me to go over to one of the men to ask them to give him a haircut. I was laughing at him but I went and asked all the same and he got his haircut. I waited two or three hours there that day," Sally recalled.

Like Winnie, Sally has fond memories of her brother.

"He was a character. When he'd come visiting us in Tuam, he was always smiling and laughing, he wasn't a bad person. You'd always have to make the tea as soon as he'd come in and he'd tell us a load of stories about things that happened years ago. He was just like any brother would be. He'd always be there for you and if you needed to talk or anything, he'd always come running," she said.

Sadly, when Sally visited John in hospital that day, it was the last time she or any of her siblings would see him alive. When Winnie eventually realised that John had been receiving treatment in the Psychiatric Unit, she was shocked.

"I was really surprised. He was always healthy out, he was always on the go, making his living and caring for his kids. John loved to visit people and I was often in bed in the morning when he'd come and knock on the door. He'd always have a happy face and was always good fun. I never knew he had a depression problem. Anytime I ever saw him, he was always happy out; happy and well," Winnie noted.

John was the trickster in the Ward household. He was the one in the family who would always entertain the others and make them forget their worries.

"If you were in the worst humour, he'd make you laugh. If you were crying, he'd make you laugh. He'd make you laugh even if you didn't want to laugh.

He'd sing 20 songs in the one song, adding his own words along the way. He was a great brother and it bugged me when he didn't come around.

When I'd call his phone, Marie would tell me he was out doing something and she'd get him to call me back but there was no ringing. Later, I found out he was wondering what was going on; wondering why none of us were visiting him in hospital. If Marie had told us, we could have gone to see him and found out what was going on. She was keeping everything so secretive. I never knew he had a depression problem. Anytime I ever saw him, he was happy as a lord and fully content," she said.

Throughout the last 10 years – and indeed prior to his death – John has been predominantly referred to in the media as 'Frog' Ward but it's a tag his family aren't happy about.

"It was a nickname that was put on him when he was a child. I think it was because he was low-set and stocky. I don't know who put it on him," Winnie noted.

"When we were kids, I often called it to him myself and many the kick I got for it! When he died, it was 'Frog' that the papers went with. He was baptised John and John was his name," she stressed.

Agreeing, Sally said she hates to see his nickname used.

"We never called him Frog, it was a nickname he had as a child and now that's what he's known as. If somebody refers to him as 'Frog' Ward when they're talking to me, I'd be always thinking 'who?' – I knew him as John and that's who he was. John was a character, always smiling. He had a lovely side-smile, I can still picture that smile," Sally added.

Chapter 4
The Early Part of 2004 for Nally and Ward

It would be difficult to find two characters with more contrasting backgrounds than Padraic Nally and John Ward. Nally has spent his life immersed in country living. The bachelor farmer has enjoyed a simplistic lifestyle in a small country cottage in rural South Mayo. Ward, on the other hand, spent his life as a career criminal. He carried with him a string of previous convictions for larceny and assault, among others.

When the two men met in Padraic Nally's farmyard in October 2004, a fight broke out and blows were exchanged. Shots were fired and a man was killed. In the immediate aftermath, as news of a killing in Funshinaugh began to spread, one would have been forgiven for surmising that it was the farmer who had lost his life.

Nally had never been in trouble with the Gardaí and was described by many as a 'quiet and decent' man. These terms could never have been used to describe the intruder he met at his back door on that cold October afternoon.

John 'Frog' Ward was well known to Gardaí across the region. He was a thief and a bully but his list of previous convictions would suggest he wasn't a particularly skilful criminal. Ward's crime spree began in his teens and he had been convicted of more than 80 crimes, spending several periods behind bars. If crime had been his career of choice, perhaps a change of direction would have been worth considering.

The early part of 2004 was very different for the two men. Nally was attempting to deal with a fear so great that it had taken over his life. His every waking moment was spent on edge. He had been targeted by thieves once too often and he was convinced he would be found dead in his bed. The farmer had become increasingly paranoid every time he saw a strange car in the area. He was constantly looking for signs of intruders at his property and he had stopped attending marts in the area, afraid of what might greet him when he would return home.

In contrast, prior to his death in October 2004, John Ward was awaiting a number of court appearances for various offences. On May 15 that year, Ward had produced a slash-hook and threatened members of the Gardaí during an incident at Carrowbrowne Halting Site on the Headford Road in Galway.

He was subsequently arrested and charged with a number of offences, which included possession of an offensive weapon and being drunk and disorderly in a public place. Moreover, at the time of his death, there were no fewer than four bench warrants out for his arrest for charges relating to theft, criminal damage and offences under the Firearms and Offensive Weapons Act.

Before coming face-to-face with John Ward on his farm in Funshinaugh on October 14, 2004, Padraic Nally's home had been targeted by criminals three times that year. On these occasions, the farmer had numerous items stolen. The entire village had been in turmoil for some time over the ongoing spate of robberies in the area and the incident at Nally's home on October 14 only served to heighten these fears.

In February 2004, intruders had broken into Nally's house and taken a chainsaw from the back bathroom. His dressing table and that of his sister had been upended and the dresser in the kitchen ransacked. His shot gun was kicked under his bed. Nally was sure it had been stolen and it was only a couple of weeks later that he discovered it under his bed.

Padraic had become increasingly worried for his safety since the spring of 2004 and said he was petrified somebody would break into the house and 'bust' him up.

Following the break-in at his house in February, he had moved his gun to the shed behind the house. He was afraid to keep the weapon in his bedroom – where it had always been – in case it would be used on him during a raid.

As the year progressed, Nally's fears intensified and towards the end of September, he started to become so concerned for his safety that he was spending four or five hours per day sitting in the shed, beside his gun, in order to guard his premises.

"I figured that if I heard anybody coming into the yard, I'd shoot over their heads and scare them away," he said.

Nally's farm work was suffering as a result.

"I had become so obsessed with these fears that my land, stock and turf had been neglected. I had turf for bringing home and sheep for shearing but I just couldn't get to it. If I was at the mart, I'd be rushing home."

The farmer – who lived alone and with turf-fires as the only heat source in his small bungalow – was so worried about further attacks on himself and his property that he had started to take down number plates of any strange cars he would see in the area. He began to make notes of registration plates and when the Gardaí searched the farmer's house after the shooting, they found registration numbers scrawled on scraps of paper and envelopes all around the house.

In May 2004, Padraic had taken note of a red Daihatsu Charade that had pulled into his yard at great speed.

"I was in the yard at the time with Joe Concannon – a neighbouring farmer – and the car was coming down the road at about 70 miles per hour. It slowed down very fast and took a sharp left into my yard. The driver leaned out the window to ask me directions to the lake and then the guy in the passenger seat leaned out his window and asked me the same thing. I knew they weren't really looking for the lake. They were surprised to see anyone in the yard," he said.

Padraic asked Joe Concannon to follow the car to see where they would go but Mr Concannon soon lost the red Daihatsu. When they later checked the registration number with the Gardaí, they found the car had been displaying false number plates.

During his trial, Mr Nally told the court that on October 14, 2004, he once again came face-to-face with the driver of the Daihatsu – a man he now knew as Tom Ward, the son of the deceased. Tom Ward denied he had ever been at the property.

According to Mr Nally, he had also come into contact with John Ward prior to October 14. Towards the end of September, Nally saw a black Ford pulling up on the road outside his house. The car reversed into his driveway. "The driver, who I now know to be John Ward, called me over and asked me if I thought it would be a good day for fishing. I was very suspicious because I didn't like the look of him and he didn't seem to have any fishing gear in his car," he said.

Padraic had become so worried and alarmed about people calling to the house in his absence that he had taken to throwing a bucket of water on the clay at the front gate and around the yard so that he could see if anybody was on his property while he was away.

"I'd look for footprints or tyre tracks in the clay and often, I'd find that people had been calling around while I was out."

In the weeks and months prior to the death of John Ward, Padraic had been unable to sleep properly at night and had always been rushing home from the mart or from his herding, fearful that his house would be targeted by thieves.

The only time he had some comfort was when his sister, Maureen, would come to stay at the weekends.

"My mind would be eased that someone was there with me but when she'd leave I'd be scared for the week. I'd be living in fear the rest of the time. I thought I would be found dead like the Gilmores in Kilmaine – they were saying their rosary at home and were broken into for money," he recalled.

The five months prior to the shooting were 'unbearable' for Padraic and on the Sunday night before the incident, when his sister had returned to her own home after the weekend, the then 60-year-old farmer sat down by the fire and cried.

"I started crying. I knew something was going to happen to me that week. I had a premonition and I thought I'd never see my sister again."

In the weeks leading up to the shooting, his life in turmoil, Padraic had only been sleeping for an hour or two each night.

"I knew something was about to happen. I thought I'd either be found dead after a raid or I'd have to shoot myself the following weekend. I couldn't take it any longer," he said.

On October 13, the night before the shooting, Padraic only slept for one hour.

Meanwhile, John Ward was living the only life he knew. The 42-year-old – a man of approximately 5ft 8in, of moderately heavy build, with receding short brown hair and tattoos on his arms and on the backs of his fingers – was ultimately an inveterate criminal who had turned his back on the norms of a civilised society. John lived his life according to his own brutal dictum and his arrival in Cross that day was, undoubtedly, part of a criminal enterprise.

During the Nally trial, not even the prosecution team could deny Ward's intentions. Nonetheless, their case was consistent insofar as it had been summed up in the opening statement by Mr Paul O'Higgins, Senior Counsel for the prosecution.

"John Ward wasn't necessarily at Mr Nally's house for the sake of the good of the community on October 14, but the penalty for larceny is not death," he told the court.

In contrast, Senior Counsel for the defence, Mr Brendan Grehan, pointed out the differences between the two men.

"John and Tom Ward came to Mr Nally's house and it would be hard to find a greater contrast than that which existed between these two men and Mr Nally," said Mr Grehan.

Backing up this statement, Mr Grehan spoke of John Ward's accumulative convictions and the fact that the deceased man had been obsessed with getting revenge on someone who had attacked him in the past. Furthermore, he reminded the jury that John Ward had been on a cocktail of drugs, legal and otherwise, when he confronted Mr Nally.

The fact of the matter – and one of the main issues raised by the Nally trial – was that John Ward should never have arrived at Padraic Nally's farmyard. He was only able to do so because of the extraordinarily lenient bail laws that seem to apply in the courts system in Ireland. John Ward should not have been at liberty to enter Padraic Nally's farmyard in October 2004; he should have been in jail.

In the immediate aftermath of the shooting – and indeed after the trial and retrial – calls were made for the then Justice Minister, Michael McDowell to address the issue of lenient bail laws as a matter of priority because these laws were contributing greatly to the undermining of public confidence in the judicial system.

In addition to his regular crime spree, John Ward was suffering with mental health issues prior to his death in 2004.

In fact, on the morning of his shooting, he had attended a day-care appointment in the Psychiatric Department at the University College Hospital in Galway.

His son Tom, who was with him in Cross that afternoon, had driven him to hospital that morning. According to Tom, his father 'wasn't well and was on a lot of medication'.

What Tom claimed he didn't know, however, was that John Ward had been hearing voices, telling him to kill himself and his wife. Of course, Tom's memory was somewhat selective in court because he also denied that his father was a violent man and said he had no knowledge of his father being involved in bare-knuckle fighting.

In fact, when some of John Ward's convictions were listed to his son in court – including the incident where he threatened Gardaí with a slash-hook – Tom claimed he wasn't aware of the majority of the offences. It later emerged Tom had been with his father when the slash-hook was brandished at Gardaí.

Prior to his death, John Ward had spent some time in the care of the Psychiatric Department at the University College Hospital in Galway. Ward was an in-patient in the Psychiatric Department from September 3 to September 21 that year. He had been readmitted on October 1 as an emergency and remained in hospital until October 12.

The Senior Registrar in the Psychiatric Department at the hospital, Dr Dymphna Gibbons, confirmed to the court during the initial trial in Castlebar that Ward had been 'hearing voices' for some time. He was also experiencing hallucinations and was often depressed.

"He told me there was a male voice in his head and it was commanding him to kill himself and his wife. Mr Ward had a difficult temper and he told me that he had lost it many times," explained Dr Gibbons.

Continuing, she confirmed that Mr Ward had a history of bare-knuckle boxing and said the deceased had told her he had inflicted serious injuries on people in the past. Mr Ward had talked to the doctor about an incident where he had been assaulted with a Stanley knife.

"He was not satisfied that his attacker had been handed down a suspended sentence and he told me that if he ever met his attacker again, he would kill him," said the psychiatrist.

Mr Ward had been a patient of Dr Sheila O'Sullivan, Consultant Psychiatrist, for some time and he told her he was quite frightened of his own 'difficult' temper.

"He was afraid of what he might do to people and thought he would attack before he was attacked," she stated.

An autopsy on the body of John Ward revealed he was ingesting a veritable cocktail of drugs – both legal and illegal – at the time of his death. Of course, when John Ward entered Padraic Nally's farm on October 14, 2004, he was still on medication from the hospital but the toxicology report showed he had opiates, cannabis and tranquilisers in his body when he died. Not all of these drugs had been prescribed.

Chapter 5
The Gilmore Brothers

The early 1980s saw the dawn of a new era of crime in rural Ireland. An economic recession had hit the country and break-ins and burglaries had become common place. In South Mayo and North Galway, the situation was no different but when an elderly spinster and two bachelor brothers were savagely attacked in their homes one week before Christmas in 1981, it was a step too far.

One of the men died at the scene of the crime at Thomastown, just outside the village of Kilmaine in Co Mayo, on December 19, 1981. A second man died in hospital a fortnight later as a result of injuries received in the attack. The woman, who was attacked in her home near Caherlistrane in Co Galway, died in hospital three months later.

On that fateful evening, four men – Martin Ward of Cuilleen, Headford; James Cleary of 2 Kildun, The Neale; Charlie Conroy of 2 Bog Road, Ballinrobe; and Eddie Conroy of 2 Bog Road, Ballinrobe – broke into Mary Connell's home at Mirehill, Caherlistrane, Co Galway. Ms Connell was to be their first victim that evening.

The 83-year-old had never married and lived alone in a small thatched cottage in rural North Galway. She was vulnerable and an easy target for the mindless thugs. The men were hoping that the spinster – like so many others at that time – would have bundles of cash stored in biscuit tins and jars around her cottage.

Ward, Cleary and the two Conroys were looking for an easy earner and didn't care that Mary Connell was a frail old woman who wasn't going to put up a fight. They were bullies and were willing to use any level of force necessary to get information – and cash – from their victim.

The four broke into Mary Connell's home at around 8pm, shouting and demanding cash. When she insisted she had nothing to give them, the 83-year-old was struck by Cleary. When she fell, she was lifted off the floor, tied to a chair by the flex of a kettle and grabbed by the hair. Mary Connell was beaten to within an inch of her life.

The men demanded money but when their demands proved unfruitful, they fled the scene, leaving her tied and slumped on the chair.

Giving evidence during the trial of Eddie Conroy and Martin Ward, a neighbour of the victim, Miss Patricia Murphy, told the court she found Mary Connell in her yard. She was tied by the neck and legs to a kitchen chair with electric flex and had blood all over her face.

Charlie Conroy, in an unsworn statement during his trial at the Central Criminal Court, admitted the dreadful act. He told Mr Justice Gannon and the jury of one woman and 11 men that he had been drinking that evening and he, his younger brother Eddie, his brother-in-law James Cleary, and Martin Ward, decided to rob Mary Connell.

"I did not know at that stage there was going to be any violence. But extreme violence was used. I hit her and James Cleary hit her with the handle of a brush," he said.

Sentencing Conroy at his initial trial in Dublin, Mr Justice Gannon described the two attacks as brutal and savage incidents.

"They were contrived to create great terror to the victim. They were terrorist-type objectives," the judge added.

Mary Connell died in hospital three months after the vicious assault but while the four men were charged with assault and intent to steal at her Caherlistrane home, no charges were ever brought forward in relation to her death as there was no conclusive evidence that Ms Connell's death was linked to the dreadful condition in which she had been left.

When the men left Mary Connell's house empty-handed on December 19, they weren't happy to cut their losses and call it a night. Consumed with greed, they decided to try their luck elsewhere. Just over the Mayo border in Shrule, they stopped and purchased four pairs of women's tights to make masks for another raid.

Then it struck them. The Gilmore brothers in Thomastown would definitely have cash in the house. They knew that for a fact.

"The Gilmores lived in Thomastown, less than half-a-mile outside Kilmaine on the road linking Kilmaine and Roundfort in South Mayo," recalled retired Detective Garda John Clancy, who was involved with the investigation.

"Earlier that day, the lads had called to the Gilmores. They used to go around selling gates, cheap slabs of timber and wooden stakes. They had called to the four Gilmore brothers in their two-storey house that afternoon and the elderly brothers had purchased some timber stakes."

That evening, it didn't occur to the gang at first to return to the Gilmores in Mayo, but when they had no success in Mirehill, they figured it was time to pay the elderly brothers a little visit. Of course, when it came to paying for the stakes earlier that day, one of the Gilmore brothers had simply gone to another room and returned with the cash. It was obvious there was more where that came from.

As it turned out, two of the four Gilmore brothers – John and Michael – had gone visiting some neighbours that night. It was a week before Christmas and a time when, traditionally, people in the countryside make their seasonal visit to friends and neighbours, picking up a 'Christmas drink' here and there.

When the four masked men burst in on Edward and Peter, they had no weapons in tow but were prepared to improvise.

"They smashed the furniture and beat them with the legs of chairs and solid planks of wood. The level of violence was shocking," recalled Mr Clancy.

Sadly, it was the dawning of a new era in rural Ireland and a sign of things to come.

"There would have been a lot of burglaries in the area and across rural Ireland around this time, but this was the start of the really vicious attacks on the elderly. Prior to that, it was mostly sneak attacks, where houses would be broken into while people were in bed or out at bingo.

This was a whole other story. There hadn't been this level of full-on violent confrontation before this and it shook the community hard."

The retired detective, who was based in Claremorris at the time, said he'll never forget the scene that greeted Gardaí in Thomastown. "When we went into the kitchen that night, it was like a slaughter house. The place was destroyed. There was blood splattered on ceilings and on walls."

When Michael and John Gilmore arrived home shortly before 10pm on December 19, 1981, they were not prepared for what they were about to find. During the trial of Edward Conway and Martin Ward – one of many protracted hearings associated with the case – the surviving brothers gave emotional evidence from the stand.

Michael Gilmore told the Central Criminal Court that one of his brothers died in his arms after he found him and a second brother lying in pools of blood in their home. The four men were charged with murdering 79-year-old Edward Gilmore. The other victim, 68-year-old Peter Gilmore, died in hospital a fortnight after the attack.

Giving evidence, John Gilmore said he was shocked to find the doors open and the upstairs lights switched on when he arrived home that evening. When he walked through the front door of his home, he saw blood on the wall. Peter was lying in a pool of blood on the floor. Edward was in a similar condition under the stairs.

Peter had been beaten and kicked by the raiders. He had fallen to the ground and did not get up. When Michael and John arrived home, both brothers were still alive. But only just. Peter asked for a drink and John fetched it for him. Edward was breathing heavily and did not respond to his brothers' attempts to speak with him.

Michael, meanwhile, stayed with Edward. It was obvious he was dying and after suffering such a brutal and vicious assault, Michael wanted to make sure his brother's last moments were in the arms of someone he loved. "When I got to the house, I went to Edward who was dying. I held him for four or five minutes, then he dropped away."

Edward's injuries included eight lacerations to his head, broken ribs, two broken cheek bones, a broken nose and brain damage.

Peter spent a couple of weeks in intensive care before he too died on January 3, 1982. For what? The four intruders had only escaped with a measly £170. That was the price of two lives in Thomastown. In fact, it was the price the three.

Effectively, three people were dead by the time Cleary, Ward and the two Conroy brothers were brought to trial but undoubtedly, the speed at which the case was solved was remarkable, with the four men making statements about their involvement before the Murder Squad had even arrived in Mayo, from Dublin, the following morning.

"The Caherlistrane attack was reported first and Sergeant Con McCole and the late Garda Des Kelly went out from Headford Garda Station. We were all very familiar with this gang and had been watching them for a while. Their names were mentioned very early in the investigation and when we went to James Cleary's house, outside The Neale in Co Mayo, we found blood embedded in the stitching and on the soles of one of his boots," recalled retired Detective Clancy.

"That time, there was no DNA testing; you just had to rely on a sample telling you it was human blood. James Cleary's defence was that he had killed a turkey for Christmas and it was turkey blood on his boot but we knew he was lying and we were adamant those responsible for these horrific attacks would pay the price."

The four suspects were rounded up and a local investigation team put in place. The men were 'invited' to attend Claremorris Garda Station for questioning because at the time, prior to the introduction of Section 4 of the Criminal Justice Act 1984, Gardaí – bizarrely – did not have the power to arrest a suspect for detention, unless he or she was being arrested and charged.

"There was no power of arrest and no periods of detention. You had to 'invite' suspects to the station. If somebody got up and walked out, they were free to go. You couldn't stop them. You couldn't detain a person to gather evidence. You only had power of arrest for the purpose of charging. An 'arrest' was only possible when you were able to hand somebody a charge sheet," explained Mr Clancy.

Fortunately, from the point of view of solving crimes, the majority of criminals weren't aware of the lack of power held by Gardaí at the time and therefore presumed they were being officially arrested for questioning.

The Gardaí, however, didn't have the same luxury with the legal teams. They, of course, knew the law inside out and during the trials into the Connell and Gilmore cases, the question of how the four men arrived at the station was raised on a number of occasions.

Needless to say, it was a ridiculous situation that Gardaí could not technically arrest a suspect for questioning in order to build a case, or indeed to rule a particular suspect in or out of an investigation as appropriate.

"There was a huge issue during one of the trials because the barrister wanted to know how his client ended up going to the Garda station. You couldn't just arrest someone to take them in for questioning and you couldn't detain them like is done now for investigations. That was a big problem at the time," said retired Detective Clancy.

Of course, the introduction of Section 4 – and not before time – allowed Gardaí to arrest a person without a warrant if the Garda had reasonable cause to suspect the person had committed an offence. A suspect, under the 1984 Criminal Justice Act, can be taken to and detained at a Garda station for an initial period of six hours. This period can be extended by a Garda superintendent.

"It was really as a result of this case and the arguments put forward by the defence teams that led to the tying up of this loophole. We were lucky we got the admissions in this instance. There was a gaping hole in the law and when Section 4 was introduced, at last we had the power to arrest, photograph, fingerprint and gather evidence."

Fortunately, despite not having the power to simply arrest the men for questioning, the Gardaí managed to round-up their four suspects and 'invite' them to Claremorris Garda Station in Co Mayo.

"We brought them to the station in Claremorris and started interviewing them. Three of them made statements of admission that night," said Mr Clancy.

The Murder Squad were due in Mayo on Sunday morning, December 20, and the investigation team already had admissions from Martin Ward, James Cleary and Eddie Conroy. "We needed the last one and we knew he was involved. A few of us decided to go in early the next morning and question Charlie Conroy again. He was the oldest and we figured he was the leader. He wasn't budging the first night but when we got chatting to him on Sunday morning, he made the admission."

When the Murder Squad arrived in Mayo, all fresh-faced and ready to take over the investigation, they were handed the four statements of admission. The case was solved.

Community policing had a large part to play in solving the crime so quickly, according to Mr Clancy.

"It was a very different set-up at the time. There was a sergeant and four or five Gardaí based in Ballinrobe and a sergeant and maybe three Gardaí in Headford, 15 miles up the road. In between the two towns, you had a sergeant and at least one Garda in Kilmaine and the same in Shrule.

"There were a lot of Gardaí around at the time. The case would never have been cracked so quickly if the level of policing wasn't there. The idea of a murder being committed at 9pm, reported a few hours later, and practically solved by 1am was fair going. We had the hard work done for the Murder Squad. The men had admitted to both incidents," he recalled.

Technically, if Ward, Cleary and the two Conroys knew the law well enough to realise they could not be arrested and were free to leave the Garda station at any time, there may never have been prosecutions for the heinous crimes.

"If the men won the argument in court and proved they were at the Garda station illegally, their statements would have been admissible. In saying that however, the level of outcry there would have been if these guys were allowed walk free after committing such horrible crimes, would have been unbelievable. Effectively, three people were dead by the time they came to trial – the two Gilmores and Mary Connell in Caherlistrane," Mr Clancy explained.

While the power of arrest issue was not a new difficulty for Gardaí, it was the first time a legal team had argued the point in court.

"The arrest issue never came up prior to that but the barristers were on the ball during the various trials. That was the first time the 'invitation' and 'power to detain' came up in court and thankfully, after that, it led to changes in the law."

***

In January 1982, the four accused – Martin Ward, James Cleary, Charlie Conroy and Eddie Conroy – were charged with the murder of Edward Gilmore. They were also charged with assaulting Mary Connell, with intent to rob her, and with entering the home of the Gilmore brothers, with intent to steal.

In July that year, James Cleary was jailed for life by Mr Justice Finlay at the Central Criminal Court in Dublin for murdering Edward Gilmore at his home. He also got 15 years for assaulting Mary Connell. He got 10 years each on separate charges of breaking into the Gilmore and Connell homes.

Cleary had denied all charges but on the conclusion of the prosecution's case, he pleaded guilty to the assault and breaking and entering charges. The jury of eight men and four women took an hour to reach a verdict on the murder charge and Justice Finlay said there was only one sentence: penal servitude for life.

The crimes were of the most savage and brutal type, ruthlessly carried out, with no element of anger or sudden temper, he added. After sentencing, prison officers and Gardaí handcuffed Cleary and hurried him out of the crowded courtroom, amid emotional scenes from his family and friends.

In December 1982, the jury at the murder trial of Edward Conroy and Martin Ward failed to reach a verdict after six-and-a-half-hours of deliberations. It was the fifth day before Mr Justice Barron. Conroy and Ward were also charged with entering the Gilmore home with intent to steal, assaulting Ms Mary Connell and entering her home with intent to steal. They denied all charges.

During the trial, Detective Garda Michael Devanney of Castlebar said that when he arrived at the Gilmore home, just after 11pm on December 19, he found the place 'in a shambles'. All the furniture was broken. He tried to comfort Peter, who asked for a drink and complained of the cold. Edward appeared to be dead.

State Pathologist, Dr John Harbison, said he performed a post-mortem examination on the body of Edward Gilmore. There were six or seven injuries to the head and damage to the brain, which was caused by blows from a blunt, straight object. This could have been the leg of a chair, he added.

There were also wounds on the hands, which were consistent with the dead man warding off blows or striking his assailant.

On the stand, Eddie Conroy said he had been brought into Garda stations on a number of occasions prior to this.

"Any time I am brought into a station, I'm not allowed to ask questions. It's the Gardaí who ask the questions," he said.

Conroy told the court he was put into a cell at Claremorris Garda Station that night and gave evidence of being pushed from one Garda to another during questioning. He claimed that during one interview, he was made stand in his bare feet in a pool of water. He also claimed one Garda pushed him against the wall and he banged his head. He said he hadn't slept all night and eventually agreed to make a statement.

Cross-examined by Mr Vincent Landy, Senior Counsel for the prosecution, Conroy said he did not ask at any stage why he was in the station. He claimed he did not complain about the bang on his head because he thought there was no point.

Conroy agreed with Mr Landy that he made an eight-page statement, all of which, with the exception of one sentence, was dictated by him. Mr David Butler, Senior Counsel for Conroy, said his client had been pushed between two Gardaí and then thrown against the cell wall. The Gardaí denied all suggestions of ill treatment.

Garda Seamus Gallagher, who was on duty in Claremorris Garda Station when the accused men arrived into the station, said they did not appear to be under any restraint. Sergeant Paul McWalter gave evidence of taking a statement from Conroy at 4.20am on December 20. He said the statement was voluntary and no threats had been made to Conroy.

Sergeant Con McCole, who took a statement from Ward in Claremorris Garda Station at 1.30am on December 20, said the statement was made voluntarily and no inducement was made. He noted that up to the point where Ward made the statement, he would have been free to leave the station at any time he wished, but he had not indicated that he wanted to leave.

The jury failed to reach a verdict in December 1982 but, during a retrial the following year, both Eddie Conroy and Martin Ward were convicted of the manslaughter of Edward Gilmore; of assault on Mary Connell; and of entering the homes of their victims with intent to commit burglary.

There was nothing straightforward about recording a conviction in the case of Charlie Conroy.

In January 1984, Conroy was sentenced to life imprisonment for the murder of Edward Gilmore. The jury at the Central Criminal Court in Dublin took just under two hours at the end of a seven-day trial to return a verdict that Conroy – a father-of-four – was guilty of the murder of Edward Gilmore; of assaulting Mary Connell, with intent to rob her, at her home in Caherlistrane; and of entering the homes of his two victims with intent to steal.

Mr Justice Gannon said he was obliged to impose a sentence of penal servitude for life on the murder conviction.

On the stand, Conroy gave evidence of arriving at the Gilmore home in Thomastown. He told the court that a big man answered the door and a struggle followed.

"I hit the man once. James Cleary hit him a few times on the top of the head with a stool. Eddie Conroy and Martin Ward knocked down Edward Gilmore and James Cleary hit him with a stool."

Conroy said the other man, bleeding very badly from the top of the head, went upstairs. When he returned, he handed over the cash. Shortly afterwards, Conroy noticed Edward Gilmore lying at the bottom of the stairs.

At the request of the defence, Mr Justice Gannon postponed sentencing on the other counts to January 27 to allow Conroy's wife to travel to Dublin to give evidence of his character. The postponement didn't serve to lessen the implications for Conroy. He was jailed for a further 12 years for entering the Gilmore and Connell homes, with intent to steal, and 12 years for assaulting Mary Connell with intent to rob her on the same date.

In court, Superintendent Vincent Smith said: "In isolated country places old people are terrified now. There is something of a rash breaking into houses occupied by older single people and taking advantage of them to steal."

Sentencing Conroy, Mr Justice Gannon described him as the brains behind the 'terrorist-type' attacks.

"They were contrived to create great terror to the victim. They were terrorist-type objectives. I am convinced you were the brains behind the operation and the leader of the violence."

Mr Justice Gannon refused leave to appeal but in August 1986, the Supreme Court quashed the conviction – by a four-to-one majority – and ordered a new trial for Charles Conroy. In his judgement the Chief Justice, Mr Justice Finlay, concluded that the interests of justice in criminal trials with a jury would best be served by a return to the old procedure, where a judge would hear submissions in the absence of a jury and rule on their admissibility.

Conroy was freed on bail on his own surety of £1,000 and one independent surety of £4,000 (or two of £2,000 each). Mr Justice Hamilton refused to accept Mr Conroy's brother, Francis, because he was on bail himself on a charge of breaking and entering at a public house.

£4,000 was subsequently lodged in the bank in Ballinrobe in the name of Mr Conroy's brother-in-law, who was an acceptable bailsman.

In February 1987, Charlie Conroy (36) was sentenced to penal servitude for life for the manslaughter of Edward Gilmore and 12 years imprisonment for the burglary of Mary Connell.

Sentencing Conroy, Mr Justice MacKenzie said: "In my 40 years of practice, I have never heard of more brutal crimes. They were revolting, cowardly and appalling. Consider public feeling when old people are beaten up and robbed in their own homes. Public opinion must be taken into account. I must be cognisant of public opinion and it is the duty of the courts to reflect that opinion."

It was the third time Conroy had been brought to trial in relation to the death of Gilmore. In the first trial the jury failed to agree on legal issues regarding his detention. He was convicted of murder in the second trial and sentenced to penal servitude for life. Conroy was subsequently granted bail and a retrial ordered by the Supreme Court when doubts were cast on the legality of his detention at Claremorris Garda Station because, although he had requested to be allowed sleep in an unlocked cell, his shoes had been taken from him.

On the stand during his final trial at the Central Criminal Court in Dublin, Conroy said he had a lot of drink taken on the day of the two incidents.

"I hope the Gilmores and the relations of Mary Connell will forgive us. It is a thing I'll never forget. It will be on my conscience the rest of my life," he told the court.

The savage and brutal attacks on Mary Connell and the Gilmore brothers in December 1981 sent waves of fear and anxiety across rural communities all over Ireland.

In South Mayo and North Galway, these cowardly and horrendous crimes have never been forgotten and when Padraic Nally took the stand at the Central Criminal Court – sitting in Castlebar – in July 2005, he told the court he had been petrified in his home.

The only time Padraic Nally had any level of comfort was when his sister, Maureen, came to stay with him at weekends.

"My mind would be eased that someone was there with me but when she'd leave I'd be scared for the week. I'd be living in fear the rest of the time. I thought I would be found dead like the Gilmores in Kilmaine – they were saying their rosary at home and were broken into for money," he recalled.

Mr Nally went on to tell the court that the five months prior to the shooting of John 'Frog' Ward at Nally's farm in Mayo were 'unbearable' and said that on the Sunday night before the incident, when his sister had gone back to Foxford after her weekend, he had cried.

"I started crying. I knew something was going to happen me that week, I had a premonition and I thought I'd never see my sister again," he told the court.

Chapter 6
Padraic Nally's Murder Trial

On Tuesday July 12, 2005, Padraic Nally's murder trial began at the Central Criminal Court, sitting in Castlebar Courthouse in Co Mayo. It was the first time in almost a century that a trial of such significance was held in the county – the last murder trial in Mayo was in July 1910 – and because of the historical importance of the occasion, Mr Justice Paul Carney broke with normal court protocol and allowed television cameras and photographers access to his courtroom.

Mr Justice Carney pointed out it was the first time since the foundation of the State that such a trial had taken place in Mayo, noting the Central Criminal Court now had the capacity 'to give a rapid trial locally'.

A major investment in the Court Services in Mayo had seen Castlebar Courthouse refurbished and extended in a €13 million facelift, enabling the trial to be held there.

"It goes without saying that it would not be possible to hold such a trial in Mayo but for the fact that we have invested so much in bringing our courthouse up to standard," Mr Fintan Murphy, County Registrar, told the court.

Mr Murphy's staff had facilitated the trial, drawing up and notifying the jury panel.

On day one of the trial, a jury was selected to hear the evidence. Mr Justice Carney praised the members for their response to the summons for jury duty. There had been one reluctant juror who asked to be excused duty on the basis that she worked in a local shop. She had earlier heard three jurors being excused because they were self-employed and another who was booked on a flight to London.

From his bench high over the well of the courtroom, the judge kindly explained that being in employment was not a sufficient reason to be excused. He told her that if she suffered any loss of pay, or any adverse treatment in respect of her working arrangements or holidays, he would bring down the full weight of his powers and court on her employer. His comments settled the matter without any further argument and the onerous duty of coming to a verdict was spelled out starkly to the jury members.

They were told by Mr Paul O'Higgins, Senior Counsel for the State, that they were the final arbiters in coming to a verdict; the judge was there simply as a referee to decide on any point of law that might arise during the trial.

The jurors, each as individuals, were the judges of the facts of the case and had to deliver their verdict in accordance with these facts.

The murder trial, with Mr Justice Paul Carney presiding, was heard before a jury of seven women and five men. Prosecuting on behalf of the state were Mr Paul O'Higgins, Senior Counsel (SC), with Mr John Jordan, Barrister of Law (BL), instructed by Mr Moran of the State Solicitor's office. The defence was conducted by Mr Brendan Grehan SC, with Mr Michael Bowman BL, instructed by Mr Sean Foy and Co Solicitors.

When arraigned before the jury on a charge of the murder of John Ward, Padraic Nally – dressed casually in a navy pullover and dark trousers – replied in a firm, even voice: "not guilty".

Outlining the case to the jury, Mr O'Higgins said the prosecution's argument would be that there was an intention of deliberate killing. The background to the case was that the accused was gravely suspicious of and disliked Travellers who stole from houses. His fear and anxiety was heightened some months before the killing when a chainsaw belonging to him was stolen from his property.

In his opening address, Counsel for the prosecution Mr O'Higgins stated: "John Ward wasn't necessarily at Mr Nally's house for the sake of the good of the community on October 14, but the penalty for larceny is not death."

Mr O'Higgins warned the jury this would not be an easy case.

"Sometimes cases, on their facts, give rise to emotions. This is not a trial about burglary; it's about the law. The law protects my life and your life. You, as the jury, have an obligation to the law. The law is how it is. You cannot re-write it," he said.

***

One of the first witnesses in the trial was Tom Ward, son of the deceased, who had been with John 'Frog' Ward on the farmyard of Padraic Nally on that fateful October afternoon in 2004. Tom told the court he had been living at Carrowbrowne Halting Site on the Headford Road in Galway for three-and-a-half-years. He left primary school in sixth class to begin buying and selling old cars and scrap. On the day in question, he had been looking for a car and he and his dad went 'spinning around'.

They had called to a number of houses where they saw old cars parked before they came to a place where they saw a small white Nissan. He parked the car and stayed in it while his father went to the house to see if it was for sale. Padraic Nally came towards him as he sat in the car and Tom told him his father was gone to the house looking for the owner. Nally said "he won't be coming back".

"He went to the shed and I saw him come out with a shotgun in his hand. He walked towards the house and let off a shot. He was out of my sight but I heard it. I drove out the road and parked. I got a fright and was shocked at what happened."

Ward added that he saw the Nissan car drive off in the other direction. He went back to the house and shouted for his father but got no answer. He stopped two cars on the road asking for help, before driving to Headford where he reported the matter to the Gardaí. He returned to the scene with the Gardaí and found out 'accidentally' that his father was dead when he heard a Garda speaking to somebody on his mobile phone.

Cross-examined by Mr Brendan Grehan, SC for Nally, Ward said he would have had 10 or 15 cars in the six months prior to October 2004. He denied that he bought cars and then sold them on quickly so they could not be traced to him. "My father was murdered trying to make a living," he told the court.

Tom Ward denied he was involved in burglary. He admitted his father had been in jail 'once or twice' but said it was for 'getting out of hand, doing stupid things and breaking the law'.

Tom told the court he left the scene because he was afraid. He did not accept his father was 'up to no good'. He agreed he had been arrested on suspicion of burglary but claimed he had done nothing wrong and was doing nothing wrong on the day in question.

He was not sitting in a 'getaway' car. He had never been at Padraic Nally's house in his life and did not accept his father was 'up to anything'.

Before the court, Tom Ward had a simple story to tell. He and his father called to Nally's house to see if they could buy a car and the end result was that Nally had 'killed and murdered [his] father'.

But Mr Grehan wanted to know more. He wanted to know what business the Wards were engaged in on that day. He wanted to know was Tom the driver of the 'getaway car'; why he had not switched off the engine; why he did not register the cars he bought and sold; and who he had bought the car from the previous day. He wanted to know if Tom had been at the Nally house previously. He wanted to know about John Ward's record of previous convictions – terminology Tom said he had difficulty understanding.

He wanted to know about John's 'interest' in fishing and about his reputation for violence.

But Tom Ward's memory of such things was not as clear as his memory of the events on the day his father died at Nally's house. He had no desire to assist Mr Grehan in establishing the scenario that the Senior Counsel wished to paint of a roaming band of burglars and thieves, terrorising law abiding people in South Mayo.

Getting annoyed by repeated questioning, Tom told Mr Grehan he had answered all his questions.

"It's very hard to make you understand anything," he said.

Tom Ward did reasonably well in fencing off the lawyer's probings until he was recalled to the witness box later in the trial to give evidence of the slash-hook incident in Charlestown.

On the stand, Ward denied knowledge of an incident in Sandyhill in Charlestown a few years earlier in which his late father had been violent and threatened Gardaí with a slash-hook.

He also denied getting into a van which had been used to transport a stolen fireplace and trying to destroy the evidence. He did not recall Gardaí stopping him from doing this, nor did he recall his father trying to assault Gardaí with a slash-hook.

Asked was he not involved in two break-ins in Oranmore, Ward agreed he was there but said he had not played a part. He admitted he was also present at the scene of a break-in at Carna in Co Galway but again claimed he was not involved.

Garda Pauric Deery told the court that during his time in Swinford he had come into contact with both John and Tom Ward.

A burglary had taken place in April 2002 and he went to a Traveller encampment at Sandyhill, Charlestown with two other officers.

"It was the campsite where John Ward and his family were staying and I spoke with John and asked him if I could search his van. A fireplace had been stolen and we thought there might be some evidence in the van that could help us."

Garda Deery said 'Frog' Ward had given Gardaí permission to search his van but that his son, Tom, had climbed into the back of the van with Frog's wife and started sweeping out the back of the van, trying to get rid of any evidence.

"I pulled Tom out of the van and held him back to stop him obstructing our search. John came out of the caravan with a slash-hook and swung it at us 10 or 12 times, threatening us," said Garda Deery.

***

On the second day of the trial, State Pathologist Professor Marie Cassidy gave evidence that John Ward had been shot twice as well as suffering 10 severe blows to the head. She said the gunshot wound to the chest would have proved fatal.

This shot had penetrated Ward's chest cavity and entered the heart where the wad of the cartridge had been found. She said the injuries indicated that the shot had been fired in a downward trajectory. The cause of death was the shotgun wound to the trunk, with blunt force trauma to the head being a contributory cause.

The deceased had suffered at least 10 severe blows to the head inflicted with a long, fairly narrow and sturdy instrument, likely to be made of wood. A short wooden stick was shown to the jury and Professor Cassidy said the stick was something like the weapon that could have caused the injuries.

Professor Cassidy said the dead man would have been in a crouched position when the fatal shot was fired and the shot would have been fired from an elevated position. "The gunman was above him when the shot was inflicted," she revealed.

Continuing, she said the earlier gunshot wound to the loin area caused flesh injuries and would have been very painful but the victim would have been able to move. She added that the fractures to the left arm may have been caused as the deceased tried to protect himself from the assault.

Detective Garda Laura Bolger from the Mapping Section of the Garda Technical Bureau provided a number of maps of the area. She said the distance from the cartridge bucket in the shed to the door at the back of the house was 46 metres and from the bucket to the area of the road where there was red staining – Ward's blood – was 53 metres.

Detective Garda Eoin Conway, a photographer with the Garda Technical Bureau, provided three photographs of John Ward's body, which were handed in as evidence. The photographs showed injuries to the right hip, head and face and left shoulder of the dead man.

Mr O'Higgins, prosecuting counsel, with the agreement of the defence, read into the record of the hearing a statement from Detective Garda Thomas Carey, an expert on guns, who gave estimates of the distances involved when John Ward was shot.

Detective Garda Carey concluded from the tests – carried out on cartridges similar to those used in the shooting – that the first shot was fired from a distance of not more than four yards. The fatal shot was from a distance of not more than five yards.

Michael Varley, a neighbour of Padraic Nally in Funshinaugh, was called to give evidence and said he was in his home on the afternoon of

October 14, 2004. At 2.10pm, he noticed a grey coloured car parked at Nally's house and subsequent to this, he heard a car revving. It reversed into his gateway and then drove off over the road. It was the same colour as the car he had seen outside Nally's house.

A short time later, Padraic Nally arrived in his white Nissan Sunny car and told him: "I'm in bother. I was broken into by the Travellers. One of them is shot and the other fellow fled."

Mr Varley dialled 999 and Nally spoke to the Gardaí. He told the Gardaí there was a shooting at his premises and gave his name. Nally then returned to his own house and was followed by Varley nine minutes later. On arrival, Varley looked around for the man who was shot and saw him inside the wall.

"I knew to look at him that he was dead. I didn't ask Padraic any questions."

Nally told Mr Varley he was having his dinner in the house when he heard a car revving up outside. There was a car in the gateway with a man at the steering wheel. Nally went in around the back of the house and saw the back door of his house was open. Ward emerged from the house and there was a scuffle at the back door. Nally was knocked to the ground and the deceased man had done his best to kick him 'in the stomach and private parts'. He was afraid he would be 'done for'.

Some time later, the Gardaí arrived and talked to Padraic Nally. Mr Varley saw Sergeant Carroll take a shotgun from Nally's car and put it into the boot of a Garda car. The witness added that he had known Nally most of his life and knew him to be a 'very kind, honest man'.

"If you ever wanted anything you could go to Padraic and he would leave his work there and go with you," he noted.

Continuing, he said that Nally lived alone, except at weekends when his sister came to stay. Padraic was afraid to leave his home in case it might be broken into in his absence. He had been on edge since February when there was a break-in at his home. A year before that, something else had been taken from his house.

Mr Varley told the court that when he saw a picture of John Ward in the paper after the incident, he recognised him as someone he had previously seen in the area in a Mondeo car.

He added: "I never thought the likes of this would happen. Padraic was really, really stressed out with all those people coming to his premises."

John Murphy, a stonemason who lives approximately two-and-a-half miles from Nally's house, was also called by the prosecution to give evidence.

On the day in question, he was on land at the back of the house when he heard a car pulling into his yard. A man got out of the vehicle and approached his shed. Mr Murphy shouted at the man, who he knew to be a member of the Travelling community. He came to the yard and the man – John Ward – spoke to him about stone.

He was suspicious of the men and noted the car registration number. He did not like to see them around as his new house had been broken into and a generator and some tools had been taken. The patio doors had also been broken in the burglary.

Mr Murphy said he had known Padraic Nally. He was a respected man in the area and always had a smile and a salute.

On the stand, Joe Concannon said he farmed land in the area and frequently visited Padraic Nally. He was in Nally's yard in April when a car came in at high speed. He took note of the number of the car and Padraic asked him to follow it. He did, but eventually lost the vehicle on the road.

A fortnight later, he saw the same car in the area. Two men were standing beside the car with the bonnet up and steam coming from the radiator. Mr Concannon did not know the men at the time but following the incident on October 14, 2004, he saw a photo in the paper and recognised one of the men as John Ward.

Mr Concannon said he had provided Gardaí with a list of car registration numbers he had recorded over the previous year-and-a-half. Padraic Nally would often ask him if he had seen a particular car and then provide him with a registration number.

Nally was suspicious of strange cars in the area and Concannon was also wary of some of them. He was aware a chainsaw had been stolen after a break-in at Nally's house and as time went on, he saw that Nally was becoming more and more agitated and fearful. He was a very worried man.

"Padraic is an out-and-out gentleman who never values his time. He was concerned about leaving the farm and house on the day before the shooting."

Mr Concannon added that at one stage, Nally said to him "God help me, God help me, I don't know what I'll do".

In reply to Mr John Jordan, BL prosecuting, witness agreed that Gardaí had checked out the numbers given to them and some of the cars belonged to people in the locality.

Martin Mellette was also called to give evidence and said he knew Nally very well.

He described Nally as 'a good neighbour and no trouble in the world'.

Mellette was at the Mart in Ballinrobe on Wednesday, October 13, and he called to Nally's house that evening to enquire why he had not been in Ballinrobe. Nally told him he had decided to wait around the house because he was worried about leaving his property vacant for any period of time.

***

The courtroom in Castlebar was packed by the time 61-year-old Padraic Nally took the stand on day three of the trial and he began his evidence by telling the court about his simple upbringing in the family home at Funshinaugh.

For this occasion, he was clean-shaven and had swapped his pullover for a jacket. He was supported by his friends, neighbours and representatives from the IFA.

Mr Nally spoke about burglaries at his home, which had commenced in 2001. He had enjoyed farming immensely up until then.

"I had always enjoyed farming but it got rough on me then. People were calling and taking things out of the yard."

He had become increasingly worried for his safety since the spring of 2004 and was petrified somebody would break into the house and 'bust' him up. When he would leave the house to go to Mass or to the mart, he was constantly checking his watch and rushing home for fear his house would be targeted by criminals.

Nally would also throw a bucket of water on the clay at his front gate and around his yard when he would leave the house. He would then check for footprints or tyre tracks when he returned home. He had also started writing down the registration numbers of strange cars in the area.

Mr Nally told the court he had come into contact with both John and Tom Ward before the shooting on his farm – Tom had pulled into his yard the previous May, while John arrived on his property at the end of September, he said.

The farmer had become so obsessed with his fears that his farm was suffering. He spent hours every day sitting by his gun in the shed. He wasn't sleeping properly at night and the only time he'd have some comfort was when his sister would come to visit at weekends.

Mr Nally told the court that on the night before the incident, he had only slept for one hour.

Throughout his evidence about the events of the afternoon of October 14, 2004, Padraic Nally spoke of the stress and fear he was feeling.

When he heard the car being revved in the laneway, he knew there was something untoward going on outside his home. After speaking with Tom Ward, he went to find the second man and when he saw John Ward trying to enter his home through the back door, he went to the shed for his gun.

Nally told the court he only intended to give the intruder a beating but got his gun for protection.

The weapon went off accidentally in his hand and the farmer was sure Mr Ward would panic and run for the car, but he didn't. A scuffle ensued at the back door, with both men giving it their all. Nally reached for a stick and began hitting Ward. He pushed him into a bed of nettles and then ran to the shed for more cartridges. He told the court he was afraid there were more than just Ward and his son.

"I was afraid more of them would come and try to kill me."

Nally said he remembered looking out and seeing Mr Ward running out the gate.

"I reloaded the gun and brought two extra cartridges. I ran out to the road and he was walking down ahead of me. I fired a shot and he fell to the ground. The gun was down under my arm, I didn't rise it up to shoot him. I had the gun pointing in his direction but I just wanted to frighten him. He fell on his right side. I went down to him. I knew he was dead," Mr Nally admitted.

The defendant told the court that the reason he reloaded after shooting Mr Ward was because he had intended to shoot himself.

"I never intended to shoot anyone in my life. I was sorry for doing it, it was just spur of the moment. The way I was treated, I had to protect myself," he explained.

Under cross examination by Mr Paul O'Higgins, SC for the prosecution, Mr Nally said he had been worried for some time about Travellers.

When Mr O'Higgins asked why he had attacked Mr Ward, given that he was so frightened, Nally said he felt he had to do something when he saw the Traveller in his house but stated that he just intended to give him a beating.

"I'm not denying to this court that I killed him. I was afraid he was going to kill me, I had to do something," he said.

Mr O'Higgins asked the farmer why he had told Tom Ward that the intruder 'won't be coming out'. In response, Nally said he wanted to frighten Tom so that he would be too afraid to follow him inside.

The defendant admitted to Mr O'Higgins that his 'temper was up' but claimed he just wanted to frighten the intruder so he wouldn't come back. Again, Mr Nally told the court he had been thinking about taking his own life in the week leading up to the incident on his farm and confided that if Mr Ward had gotten away uninjured that day, he would have killed himself rather than go through it all again.

"If he had gone away that day, they'd still be robbing my house and I'd be lying in my grave. I'd have killed myself, because I couldn't take any more and there'd be no court case," he said.

Mr Nally also told the court that when John Ward had called to his house at the end of September, he knew by the look of Mr Ward that he was going to kill him.

Little did the farmer realise that the opposite would occur.

***

Among the witnesses to take the stand at the hearing in Castlebar was the Senior Registrar in the Psychiatric Department at the University College Hospital in Galway, Dr Dymphna Gibbons.

Mr Michael Bowman, BL for the defence, questioned Ms Gibbons about her dealings with the deceased and she told the court Mr Ward had been in her care for some time and had been 'hearing voices'. He was experiencing hallucinations and was often depressed.

"He told me that there was a male voice in his head and it was commanding him to kill himself and his wife. Mr Ward had a difficult temper and he told me that he had lost it many times," she said.

Dr Gibbons confirmed that Mr Ward had a history of bare-knuckle boxing and said the deceased had told her he had inflicted serious injuries on people in the past. He had a number of previous convictions and was known to Gardaí.

From the witness box, Dr Gibbons said Mr Ward had talked to her about an incident where he had been assaulted with a Stanley knife.

"Mr Ward was not satisfied that his attacker had been handed down a suspended sentence and he told me that if he ever met his attacker again, he would kill him," said the psychiatrist.

Under cross-examination by Mr John Jordan, BL prosecuting, Dr Gibbons said she found Mr Ward cooperative and pleasant at all times.

"He respected my authority and that of the treatment regime."

Dr Sheila O'Sullivan, Consultant Psychiatrist at University College Hospital Galway told the court that John Ward had been a patient of hers for some time and had told her on occasion that he was quite frightened of his own 'difficult' temper.

"He was afraid of what he might do to people and thought he would attack before he was attacked," she stated.

The Consultant Psychiatrist confirmed that Mr Ward was an in-patient in the Psychiatric Department from September 3 to 21, 2004, and had been readmitted on October 1 as an emergency. He had remained in hospital until October 12.

Like the previous witness, Dr O'Sullivan told the court she had always found Mr Ward pleasant and cooperative.

"He was grateful for the treatment and was willing to comply with out-patient appointments," she said.

The court heard that the toxicology report on Mr Ward showed he had opiates, cannabis and tranquilisers in his system when he died.

Ms Maureen Nally, the only sister of the accused, was called to give evidence to the court on day four and stated that, like her brother, she had never married and still travelled to the family home every weekend to spend time with Padraic.

"I went home every Friday after work and would return to my house in Foxford after dinner on Sunday," she said.

Ms Nally told the court she had purchased the chainsaw for her brother in Killeen's of Ballina on October 1, 2003. She confirmed it had been stolen from Padraic's house in February 2004.

When asked about her brother's behaviour in the months prior to the incident, Maureen said she had noticed changes in Padraic. She pointed out that during lambing season each year, Padraic would often stay outdoors until 10pm at night attending to his chores.

"In the spring of 2004, he wasn't bothered about sheep or lambing and in July and August, he had gotten worse. Lately, I noticed he'd go to sleep on the chair after dinner on Friday and he might fall asleep again on Saturday at about 4pm and again on Sunday morning after he'd come in from herding. It was totally out of character but it was because he wasn't sleeping during the week while I was away," she explained.

Continuing, Ms Nally said her brother had started losing interest in his farm work. She also noticed that when they would come home from Mass on Saturday evenings, Padraic would always get out of the car at the gate and would be looking at the ground, checking for tyre marks or footprints.

"When the days started getting shorter in the weeks before the incident, he would go out to the gate with a torch after we came home from Mass and check the gate and the yard for evidence of intruders," she added.

Ms Nally told the Court that Padraic had also lost interest in general things and often appeared distracted.

"The Sunday of the All-Ireland Final stands out in my mind. I wanted to go back to Foxford early to watch the match and I asked him if he'd come back with me. He was very agitated and told me he couldn't leave the house. I was worried about him and when I got home, I was sorry that I had left him at all. I couldn't focus on the match," she said.

The next day, Ms Nally had to go back to Cross to attend a funeral and first called to the house to see Padraic.

"He was sitting in the chair when I came in and he appeared startled when I entered the room. He wouldn't open up about the match and had a paper in front of his face. I knew he wasn't concentrating on the paper; he was thinking about something else. We went to the funeral and when we came home, he once again checked the yard for footprints," she recalled.

On the evening of October 14, 2004, when Maureen met her brother at Castlebar Garda Station, he informed her that he had cried when she left the house the previous Sunday.

"I asked him why he cried and he told me he was very worried, anxious and fearful for his life. He thought he would never see me again," Maureen told the court.

Chapter 7
Attacks on the Elderly in Rural Ireland

Fear and terror swept rural Ireland in the early 1980s. Isolated homes were being targeted by gangs of criminals and elderly residents in small towns and villages were petrified that they would be the next victims. Random attacks for gain on the elderly became all-too-common in counties Mayo, Galway and Roscommon, among others, and Gardaí across the west of Ireland issued several warnings to vulnerable people living alone, pleading with them not to answer their doors to strangers and appealing to communities to be on the lookout for any suspicious activity in their areas.

In many cases, however, these travelling gangs didn't wait for a door to be opened, forcing entry to homes and barging their way through houses in search of cash and other valuables.

In November 1980, for instance, 87-year-old Kate Burke was bound and gagged in her home at Cloonascragh, Kilconly, outside Tuam in North Galway, when three men entered her house and demanded money. The elderly spinster was threatened with a pig-knife when she refused to tell the intruders where they could find cash. Her hands were tied with stockings and she was gagged when she tried to scream for help. The intruders proceeded to ransack Kate's home, before they located her savings.

It was 21 hours before a bloodied and frightened Kate was found by neighbours. The three men had made off with £85, after they broke into her home at around 11pm on November 4 that year.

The elderly woman, who was taken to hospital after she was discovered the following evening, was badly shaken by the incident. Her wrists were bruised and she had blood marks on her face.

One of the men, who was later convicted of robbery and assault, was originally from Belclare outside Tuam and had grown up less than one mile from her home. His accomplices were from Waterford and Cork.

Another such incident occurred in Mayo on Tuesday March 8, 1983, when two elderly brothers were terrorised in their home for up to four hours after a number of men, armed with sticks and a saw, forced entry to their home in Cashel, Foxford, and stole several hundreds of pounds.

Shortly before 8.30pm that evening, a group of men arrived at the door of the home shared by Pakie and Brian Healy. The men demanded they be let into the house and when Brian refused them entry, they smashed a hole in the door and forced their way inside.

One of the intruders grabbed Brian by the throat and threatened to kill him. Pakie, who was lying in bed at the time, was also physically assaulted when one of the robbers struck him a blow.

The men smashed chairs and furniture in the kitchen, before ransacking an adjoining room and making off with cash in the region of £600. Before leaving, the men warned the Healy brothers not to report the crime to Gardaí and told them they would return and murder them if a report was made.

It wasn't the first time Pakie and Brian had been targeted. The previous Thursday night, a group of men tried to gain entry to their home through the back door but the brothers managed to beat them away with a tongs and a poker. A couple of days after the break-in on March 8, both brothers were hospitalised.

A story on the front page of the *Western People* newspaper in December 1984, reported that Gardaí in Mayo were making a concerted effort to track down and put behind bars a gang – or gangs – who were responsible for terrorising elderly people living in remote areas.

The report noted that the campaign had been stepped up following recent incidents where force had been used to gain access to isolated homes and elderly people had been assaulted.

No fewer than six cases were under investigation in Mayo that week, with incidents in the Swinford, Belmullet, Westport, Charlestown, Kiltimagh and Knock areas. In a number of these incidents, the gangs had used force to persuade the occupants to tell them where to find money in the houses.

A Garda spokesperson had told the *Western People* that the gangs were well organised and were either spending considerable time watching their 'marks' or were being supplied with information locally.

The Gardaí also stated that they were fearful there may be other cases that had not been reported to them for a variety of reasons. There were suggestions that some elderly people might not want to report the crimes because they felt the pension officer may have an interest in their savings. Others, perhaps, did would not want neighbours to know they had been robbed.

Gardaí warned people in rural Ireland to be wary of people calling to their doors, looking for water to cool their car engines or selling carpets and blankets. They also noted there was a disturbing trend of gangs calling late at night and forcing entry into homes. The common element in all the attacks, they said, was that the victims were elderly and living in isolated areas.

***

The cowardly attacks on elderly people continued throughout the 1980s and into the 1990s. One of the more high profile cases in the west in the latter decade saw the legendary Mayo footballer Henry Dixon suffer two attacks by raiders at his Claremorris pub in the space of five days. On Monday January 9, 1995, the 76-year-old was hospitalised after raiders broke into his premises for a second time.

The first attack had occurred the previous Thursday evening when Mr Dixon disturbed a youth who was taking money from his bedroom, upstairs at his James Street premises.

Two men and another youth who were downstairs in the pub helped free the perpetrator and the raiders escaped in a dark blue Volkswagen Setanta with cash and bank notes.

Four days later, in the early hours of January 9, a gang broke into the premises and tied up Mr Dixon, assaulting him while they searched for money. They escaped in a white Nissan Sunny van.

Retired Detective Garda John Clancy, who was stationed in Claremorris at the time, was involved with the investigation and recalled the chain of events.

"I was on duty that Thursday. It was a cold, wet day and I was just driving out the Knock Road when I got a call to say there had been some trouble down in Henry Dixon's pub. I turned and went back into town and called to see him. There were a few others in the bar and when I asked Henry what had happened, he shrugged it off. He had been robbed but he didn't want to do anything about it or to report it to the Gardaí," explained Mr Clancy.

The next day, Detective Clancy visited Henry again and pleaded with the former Mayo footballer to tell him what had happened.

"Eventually, he sat down and told me that in the mid-afternoon, two men and three or four children had come in to the pub. That in itself was strange because no outsiders ever went in to Henry Dixon's. He had a group of regulars who played a few games of cards at night but no stranger ever went in. That's just how it was," he continued.

"The group had arrived, ordered a drink and the kids had asked to go to the toilet. Henry told them the toilet was out the back but instead, they went upstairs. Henry lived above the pub, three stories up, and when there was no sign of the children after a few minutes, he got suspicious and tore up the stairs. They had gone all the way up to Henry's bedroom, had found the safe, located the keys, opened the safe, and had a bag of money coming out the door. He challenged them, but they got away. By the time Henry got back down to the pub, they were all gone."

When Detective Garda Clancy asked Henry how much had been taken, he wouldn't tell him. Conscious that there was still probably a lot of money upstairs, Detective Clancy warned the publican that they might return for more money and pleaded with him to put the remainder of the cash in the bank.

"He was afraid to put the money into the bank at first – a lot of people at the time were of the same mind – but I managed to convince him. He cleaned out his safe – there was about £200,000 in it – and I brought him up the street to the bank and let him do his business."

The following Monday, Detective Clancy was on duty again when he received a report from the station that Henry Dixon had been targeted again.

"They broke into the premises, went up the stairs and found Henry in his bed. The intruders tied him to the bed – to each of the four posts – and they beat him black and blue. Henry was clever enough though, he had kept back some cash that he didn't lodge in the bank and had hidden it under the bed. Eventually, when they realised he had no more cash in the room, they took the money and went," added Mr Clancy.

Investigations led the Gardaí to Miley Connors and Ned Stokes. Miley was part of a gang from Tallaght. He was on bail and was reporting once a week to Portlaoise Prison, as per his bail conditions.

"We found out what day Connors was reporting to Portlaoise and when Henry got out of hospital, we drove him up and sat outside the prison. We asked the Governor to delay Connors outside for a few moments to allow Henry to get a proper look at him. Henry identified him as one of the men who came to the pub the first day with the kids. We had something to go on," recalled Detective Clancy.

After Gardaí arrested Connors and brought him in for questioning, he volunteered a second name, Ned Stokes who was also arrested and questioned.

At Claremorris District Court in February 1995, Michael Connors of The Square, Tallaght, pleaded guilty to assisting in the theft of £10,000 from Mr Dixon's premises, but insisted he was not present for the assault on the 76-year-old.

The following December, Ned Stokes of no fixed abode and of Belcamp Lane, Coolock, Dublin, admitted two counts of robbery on Henry Dixon on January 5 and 9, 1995. He was sentenced to 18 months imprisonment when he was convicted of robbing the former Mayo football star of €13,000.

Claremorris District Court heard that Henry Dixon was tied to his bed and beaten severely with a pool cue in the second robbery. He had been lucky to survive the attack.

Detective John Clancy stated that on January 5, Dixon was alone in this premises at Lower James Street. Two men and some children came into the pub. One of them purchased a drink and left and the other remained there.

While Mr Dixon's attention was distracted, the children went upstairs. They managed to open the safe and stole a substantial sum of money. When they were coming down the stairs, Mr Dixon challenged them. They made their way to a car, which was driven by the defendant, Ned Stokes.

Detective Clancy went on to tell the court that the next robbery took place on January 9 in the early hours of the morning. Henry Dixon was asleep in his bedroom, where the safe was located, when raiders broke into his home. He was severely beaten with a pool cue and the raiders threatened to shoot him. He was tied up and the beating went on for somewhere in the region of one hour.

Demands were made for Mr Dixon to tell the raiders the location of the keys to the safe but he refused. The court heard Henry Dixon was a strong man but eventually the raiders overcame him and tied him to the bed. They grabbed the safe and carried it down three flights of stairs. While they were loading the safe into the waiting vehicle, Mr Dixon managed to escape and alerted two people outside. One of the people later identified Ned Stokes as the man loading the safe. Mr Dixon was taken to Claremorris Garda Station and from there to Castlebar Hospital, before being transferred to University College Hospital Galway, where he was treated for his injuries. Photos of Mr Dixon after the attack were handed to the judge.

At Claremorris District Court, Detective Clancy said Dixon had made a reasonable recovery, but had suffered the loss of the sight in his left eye since the attack. The Garda investigation centred on a man called Miley Connors, who had already been dealt with. Stokes was married to one of the Connors, he said.

Continuing, Detective Clancy said, after the robbery, Stokes and other suspects went to England and stayed there for some time. He later arrested Stokes in Dublin, after he found him hiding in the wardrobe of his caravan. He was taken to Castlerea Garda Station and was identified by one of the witnesses as being at the scene of the robbery on January

9. When arrested, he refused to cooperate, but when he was charged, he mentioned the payment of compensation. He had a long list of previous convictions dating back to 1986 and was a violent man who had carried out several other burglaries.

Henry Dixon, replying to Judge Brennan, said he could only see 'a small bit' with one of his eyes since the attack. All of the money had since been recovered.

Addressing the court, Judge Brennan described incidents such as this one as 'a cancer', noting they were happening in the five counties where he sat as a judge and indeed all over the country.

"It is a terrible state of affairs that the aged who gave their life's blood to this country can't live in the tranquillity and ease to which they are entitled at this stage of their lives. I recently heard a case of an elderly woman. An auctioneer called to give her money for the letting of her land and she was so afraid, she hid under the bed," he said.

"This man has worked hard all his life and saved his money. Upwards of £10,000 has been recovered but that does not justify the means by which it was got. I cannot leave this man free and will not."

Inspector Michael Hussey called for the imposition of the maximum two-year sentence. He pointed out that only for the victim was a strong man, he might not have survived the attack. Mr Dixon had played on the Mayo All-Ireland winning team in 1950 and again in 1951. He was very lucky he wasn't suffocated, as paper had been stuffed down his throat during the attack.

Judge Brennan imposed a nine-month consecutive sentence for each of the two robberies. He said he wasn't imposing a further six months as Stokes wasn't the man who carried out the assault.

Recalling the incident, retired Detective Clancy said the attack on Henry Dixon was unusual in that it occurred in the town of Claremorris and not in the rural countryside. "There was a lot of fear generated in the town as a result. People wouldn't have expected something like that to happen. There were a lot of elderly people living around the area where the pub was located and it frightened them. We were under pressure to solve it quickly, as people were very worried. We needed to close the case fast," he said.

"It was a new departure to have such a level of violence in a town and on a man that was so well known. Henry was a big strong man and it took a huge effort on the part of the robbers to subdue him and tie him down. It wouldn't have been easy to get control of Henry and to tie him to a bed. The room was in turmoil, a big struggle had taken place. Stokes was the only one charged but there's no way he could have subdued Henry on his own, he'd have needed at least two more with him," reasoned the retired detective.

According to Mr Clancy, the attacks definitely shortened Henry's life. He never moved back to his home after the incidents, choosing to live with his sister, who ran a Bed and Breakfast on Mount Street in Claremorris.

Henry Dixon passed away in late December 1998 at the age of 81. At his funeral, he was described as the powerhouse who inspired his colleagues in the glory days of the Green and Red. Henry had only made it onto the Mayo team in his early 30s, when most would be retiring, and he went on to become something of a folk hero.

Speaking at his funeral, his nephew, Cormac Hanley said Henry never looked for plaudits. "He was always a perfect gentleman and wouldn't hurt a fly ... unless you had the misfortune to run into him on the football field."

***

Around the same time, Gardaí in County Roscommon were finding it increasingly difficult to pin-point criminals for a series of attacks on the elderly. Retired Detective Garda Basil Johnson, who was part of a Divisional Investigation Unit between Roscommon and Galway-East at the time, said the attacks were happening far too frequently and because many of the criminals were from travelling gangs, it was often hard to solve the crimes.

"We were haunted with attacks on the elderly between Roscommon and Athlone for a couple of years. People that time kept a lot of money in their homes; in biscuit tins and in jars. Thousands of pounds in cash were taken from people. These crimes were happening across the west of Ireland generally and there were a number of incidents in the Lecarrow, Knockcroghery area. It was ongoing and we were actually getting embarrassed. The annoying thing was we knew who was doing them but we couldn't prove it.

Old people were being targeted and tied up. The perpetrators would go across the fields and target a house in an isolated area where little old men and women were living," he explained.

The Gardaí knew who was responsible for a number of the crimes but were having trouble proving their suspicions.

"We spent nights hiding in bushes, trying to catch them. Eventually, there was a breakthrough and a guy called Aidan Fallon – from the Lecarrow area – was convicted of a number of attacks for gain on the elderly. He had been arrested several times before that but we didn't have enough to convict. Finally, we arrested him and brought him to Ballinasloe Garda Station. Certain things had been found in a search to connect him to one of the crimes and he eventually made a statement and admitted several of the attacks, where sums of cash had been taken. Some of the people had been badly beaten; they were ruthless attacks," recalled Mr Johnson.

In January 1998, Aidan Fallon of Rinnegan, St John's, Lecarrow, was among a number of people sentenced to prison at Roscommon Circuit Court after being found guilty of a series of crimes.

Judge Anthony Kennedy sentenced Fallon to a total of six years in prison for robbing and falsely imprisoning 69-year-old Catherine Dillon of Ballybrogan, Lecarrow on December 6, 1995, and 75-year-old Christy Doyle of Glanduff, Kiltoom, on September 12, 1995.

In addition, David Myers of Harry's Lane, Athlone and Peter McDonald of 4 Crystal Village, Athlone, were sentenced to three years for robbing and falsely imprisoning Catherine Dillon, with the last two years suspended on condition they enter a bond and keep the peace for a period of five years.

In court, Judge Kennedy noted the ages of the victims. He said the victims were known to Fallon and were targeted because of their vulnerability. On the night of the attack on Mrs Dillon, Fallon knew her son was at bingo so the time was right to strike. Mrs Dillon was in her bed when she heard a noise and figured it was her son returning home. Unfortunately, this wasn't the case. The three men cut the telephone wires, tied the old lady to a chair with sticky tape and threatened to kill her. Mrs Dillon first gave the raiders £600 and then another £139 from her purse. Envelopes containing just £1 each in dues for the clergy were ripped open by the men.

In Mr Doyle's case, he was grabbed by two men and knocked to the ground when he went outside his home to get some water at 9.25pm on the evening of September 12.

Mr Doyle's hands and feet were tied with baling twine in the attack and several threats on his life were made. When the men demanded money, he told them there was cash in his inside pocket.

The court also heard of a separate case, where an elderly brother and sister had their life savings stolen when Aidan Fallon and three others broke into their home on October 12, 1996 and made off with £20,000. The men entered the home of Michael and Annie McDermott, Mount William, Monksland in South Roscommon, at 2.30am and demanded money.

Annie McDermott's feet and hands were tied with stockings. When she broke free, she found her brother in a distressed state. One of the men had placed a lump of timber across his chest, before adding his own weight to the timber.

When one of the men found two £50 notes in a drawer, Annie told him that was all the cash they kept in the house. The raiders didn't believe this claim and the elderly woman was punched in the face. Ransacking the house, the men eventually located a total of £20,000 in cash.

In court, the Gardaí pointed out that in this particular crime, the people Fallon had gotten involved with were professionals. He had not received any of the money and was out of his depth with this gang. Fallon was sentenced to seven years in prison after he entered a guilty plea to a charge of unlawfully entering the house and stealing £20,000.

In a third case that came before Roscommon Circuit Court in January 1998, Aidan Fallon was sentenced to two years in prison for robberies at Curraghboy. The second accused in this instance – Gerard Fallon of Grange, Curraghboy – had been dealt with by the courts previously and was also sentenced to prison.

During the hearing of this case, Aidan Fallon pleaded guilty to the theft of drink from Kelly's licensed premises in Lecarrow and to taking goods from the dwellings of Frank Fallon, Thomas McKeown, John Feeley and Nancy Fallon.

Aidan Fallon was charged with entering the home of Frank Fallon at Grange, Curraghboy on March 16, 1997 and stealing £50 cash; entering the home of Thomas McKeown in Grange on March 17 and stealing five bottles of spirits, 12 cans of Heineken and a frozen ham, valued at £80; with entering Thomas Kelly's licensed premises on March 18 and stealing 24 bottles of cider valued at £60 and 24 bottles of Corky's valued at £60; with entering the dwelling of John Feeley at Coolegarry, Curraghboy, between March 31 and April 1, and stealing one frozen duck, a box of chicken pieces and one swiss-roll valued at £8.97; and on March 26, entering the home of Nancy Fallon and stealing one bottle of whiskey, one bottle of Baileys, 12 cans of Heineken and £6 cash, with a total value of £38.

The court heard the houses were grouped together in a farming locality and there was nobody in any of the houses at the time of the burglaries. In this regard, Judge Anthony Kennedy said the fact that the movement of householders in the Curraghboy area was under observation added a 'sinister element' to the crimes.

Judge Kennedy sentenced Fallon to two years in prison for this series of burglaries and ordered that the sentences be served concurrently with the seven-year term imposed for the McDermott robbery.

Chapter 8
Nally's Conviction and Sentencing

The Padraic Nally murder trial in July 2005 lasted six days in its entirety and attracted unprecedented attention from local, national and even international media organisations. Towards the end of the trial and with the final verdict imminent, interest in the case was increasing by the minute and large crowds began to descend on Castlebar Courthouse.

However, when the legal teams gathered on Tuesday July 19, to sum up their cases, there wasn't a sound to be heard in the courtroom. The accused man, Padraic Nally, sat in silence as his fate was argued upon before his very eyes.

Throughout the trial, the prosecution's case had been consistent insofar as it was summed up in the opening statement by Mr Paul O'Higgins.

"John Ward wasn't necessarily at Mr Nally's house for the sake of the good of the community on October 14 last, but the penalty for larceny is not death," he had told the court. This sentiment reverberated throughout the prosecution's case.

The conclusion of the trial also brought about a rather unusual development when Mr O'Higgins invited the trial judge to direct that the defence of self-defence should only be allowed to go to the jury 'in a truncated form, shorn of any possibility that the jury might acquit altogether'.

The Senior Counsel for the prosecution was obviously somewhat concerned that the jury might find the defendant not guilty of any crime and appealed to the judge to ensure this would not happen. Addressing Mr Justice Paul Carney, Mr O'Higgins urged the judge not to leave open the possibility that the jury might bring a complete acquittal which, he said, would "be plainly perverse".

He told the trial judge that an acquittal would be wrong "on the basis that the amount of force used was so excessive as to destroy any notion that it was objectively reasonable and that in such circumstances it should only be open to the jury to convict of either murder or manslaughter".

Taking the argument of the prosecution on board, Mr Justice Paul Carney told the jury they could only record a verdict of guilty of murder or guilty of manslaughter. The option to find Mr Nally not guilty of a crime – and to therefore acquit him altogether – was not open to them.

Addressing the jury of five men and seven women, Mr O'Higgins stated that the killing that took place would, at the very least, amount to an unlawful killing.

"There are circumstances where, even though a killing is unlawful, it will not amount to crime by murder. It falls to the prosecution to prove beyond reasonable doubt that this crime was murder," he explained.

Continuing, Mr O'Higgins told the jury that the prosecution was arguing that when Padraic Nally killed Mr Ward, "he used more force than was reasonably needed".

"Mr Nally had won the fight, it was over. The law doesn't allow someone to kill someone, just in case that someone would have come back later to kill him," he reasoned.

Mr O'Higgins went on to say that ultimately, there was very little difference in the evidence between the two parties.

"I understand that John Ward had a troubled background and had got into trouble on occasion. Similarly, I've no reason to doubt that Padraic Nally is an honest man. Mr Nally told Sergeant Carroll he had decided to 'shoot him out because [he] couldn't live with it anymore'. That move will sum up the entirety of this case," he stated.

The Senior Counsel admitted he didn't doubt that Mr Nally was concerned with people burgling his house and was worried someone might have attacked him, "but the law doesn't allow shooting or killing so that you can put them out of action for six months".

Mr O'Higgins then suggested the jury ask a number of questions of themselves. "When you consider the issues – his honest belief or his provocation – you should consider them, looking through the eyes of the accused," he said.

"Did Mr Nally decide he would finish off John Ward because he was afraid he would be attacked or killed? Do you honestly believe that the force he used was necessary? It's very hard to see that this killing was in any sense, self-defence. If you looked into Mr Nally's heart of hearts, do you think you would discover that nothing short of killing John Ward was necessary?" asked Mr O'Higgins.

Once again, the Senior Counsel for the prosecution argued that he found it hard to see the suggestion that Mr Nally "did this killing because he felt there was no other way".

"Maybe he had a general fright but did he use more force than he honestly believed was necessary in the circumstances? If you think he didn't, then you will properly find him guilty of manslaughter instead of murder," he said.

Mr O'Higgins then asked the jury to question Mr Nally's motivation to shoot John Ward. "Was he a man that hated what was happening to him and wanted to put an end to it? Did he decide that he was going to give it to the next person that arrived? Do you believe that the first shot was fired by accident or is it the fact that he decided the next person that would come to his house would get it from him? And do you feel that he was therefore moved by passion?" he queried.

Concluding his argument, Mr O'Higgins faced the jury and looking into each of their eyes, he asked: "Do you honestly believe that Mr Nally felt he needed to shoot Mr Ward? If you don't think this, then it's murder."

When Mr Brendan Grehan, Senior Counsel for the defence, stood to make his closing statement, there were a number of preliminary matters he felt he needed to outline and he explained to the jury once again that there were only two options open to them in deciding the fate of Mr Nally.

He drew on Mr O'Higgins' statement, commenting that the Senior Counsel had made much by way of speculation and attributed motives to Padraic Nally that he didn't put to him in the witness box.

"You cannot speculate where there is no evidence – from the witness box or in the exhibits. It is not enough for Mr O'Higgins to now suggest that Mr Nally did what he did on this day because he had a grievance with Travellers. Padraic did not go looking for trouble, it came looking for him," he noted.

Addressing the jury, Mr Grehan questioned whether or not they seriously believed that after 60 years, Padraic Nally had suddenly become a murderer.

"You are the jury and this case is not about whether or not civilisation is going to end because Mr Nally did what he did," he stated.

Continuing, Mr Grehan said his client had acted in self-defence and was provoked. He explained that the defence would not seek to make an insanity plea.

Addressing the men and women of the jury, he told them that for the first time in 100 years, a murder trial was being held in Mayo.

"Mr Nally is being tried by his peers – people from across the length and breadth of the county. You are representing the county and your decision will be based on your experiences and your common sense in assessing the facts," he said.

Mr Grehan assured the court that nobody regretted what had happened as much as Padraic Nally and he drew from comments made by his client after the shooting.

"In a statement to the Gardaí, Mr Nally asked about his gun and whether or not he would ever get it back again. This shows that Mr Nally was even more concerned for his safety in the immediate aftermath of what he had done," reasoned Mr Grehan.

Continuing, he said Mr Nally did not go for the gun straight away, even though he 'smelled a rat'.

"It was only when he found John Ward had busted in through his back door that he went for the gun," he explained.

Mr Grehan also reminded the jury of the Gilmore brothers in Kilmaine – one of whom was killed during a robbery involving Travellers, while a second brother died a fortnight later in hospital – and opined that Padraic Nally's fear was not irrational.

"I don't remember that particular incident but I remember lots of others. In my time in criminal law, I have learned that burglars don't tend to set out to kill people, but it happens. You are in the most mortal danger when someone comes into your house. Sometimes they act deliberately and tie them up or beat them up not intending that they'll die, but they do die. This is where Mr Nally's fears come from," Mr Grehan explained.

The Senior Counsel went on to point out that when people came to Mr Nally's house and stole from him, they took more than a chainsaw or a barrel or other goods.

"They took his peace of mind. We all crave and desire a sense of security – this had been taken from Padraic and it began to affect him in a very serious way," he remarked.

Mr Grehan then took the jury through the basic outline of his case, once more reminding them of his client's intense fear in the weeks and months before the incident at his farm. He spoke of the people who called to his house looking for the lake; Mr Nally's decision to move his gun to the shed; the noises that Mr Nally had heard; the fact that he had difficulty sleeping; the security that he felt only when his sister came to stay with him at weekends; and the fact that Padraic Nally had been seriously contemplating suicide.

"John and Tom Ward came to Mr Nally's house and it would be hard to find a greater contrast than that which existed between these two men and Mr Nally," noted Mr Grehan.

In backing up this statement, Mr Grehan spoke of John Ward's accumulative convictions and the fact that the deceased had been obsessed with getting revenge on someone who had attacked him in the past. Furthermore, he reminded the jury that Mr Ward had been on a cocktail of drugs – legal and otherwise – when he confronted Mr Nally.

Mr Grehan once again spoke of his client's fear.

"He did what he did, all the time aware that Tom, who was being called by his father, was just a little bit away in his car. We saw Tom in the witness box earlier in the trial and he's no shrinking violet. Tom has a temper – you got to see a bit of that in the witness box. Mr Nally didn't know if Tom was on his own or if he had gone to get reinforcements," he stated.

The Senior Counsel also drew on Mr O'Higgins' suggestion that Nally had shot Ward because of a grievance he had with Travellers.

"The prosecution could have chosen to put my client in the witness box and ask him this but they chose not to," he said.

Mr Grehan then recalled the evidence of Tom Ward and the fact that he had told the court he and his father had been out for a 'spin in the countryside'.

He also noted Garda Deery's evidence about the incident with the slash-hook and Tom Ward's lack of recollection of the event.

"Perhaps Garda Deery imagined the whole incident," he remarked.

Continuing, Mr Grehan stated that his client was entitled to guard his property.

"Padraic Nally reacted in the heat of the moment to a developing situation. If anything, he lost control of his mind. This man is not a murderer. He is someone that, when faced with a situation, chose not to take it lying down. Mr Nally doesn't seek to shrink away from what he did but whether he is a murderer or not is up for question – I submit that he isn't," concluded Mr Grehan.

Sending the jury out to consider their verdict, Mr Justice Paul Carney told them their options in stark terms. They could find Mr Nally guilty, or not, of murder but they did not have the 'not guilty' option on the manslaughter charge. They had to reach a unanimous verdict. If they failed to reach unanimity, there would have to be a retrial.

Six days earlier, the seven women and five men had been praised by the trial judge for their response to the summons for jury duty. Mr Nally had pleaded not guilty on the first day of the trial and was placed on a seat opposite the jury where they had a clear view of his demeanour.

Padraic Nally kept his emotions well reined in during the hearing and his demeanour remained practically unchanged.

In the middle, between the jury and the accused man were the learned counsel – Paul O'Higgins, SC for the State, supported by John Jordan BL and Mary Moran of the offices of Westport-based State Solicitor Seamus Hughes; and Brendan Grehan SC, with Michael Bowman and solicitor Sean Foy for the accused.

In front of these were the court registrar and the stenographers. Behind was a bevy of reporters, local and national, print and broadcast. It was a big occasion – the first murder trial in Mayo since the foundation of the State.

Behind the reporters were Nally's family members, friends and witnesses. Behind them, curious and interested members of the public. Over against the wall, behind and to the right of the accused man, in view of the jury whenever they wished to look, was John Ward's widow and other members of her family.

At the beginning of the trial, the jury had been warned by Mr O'Higgins that this would not be an easy case. He could not have been accused of overstating the point. The emerging evidence and the manner of its delivery, together with the sub-plots raised by the defence, guaranteed that the jury could have no doubt, reasonable or otherwise, about the difficult decision they would have to make.

On the sixth day of the hearing, the jury was sent out with little advice about how to weigh the state of the man's mind but they took two just hours and 10 minutes to reach a decision.

At 2.39pm on Wednesday, July 20, the jury returned with a unanimous verdict. They had found Padraic Nally not guilty of murder but guilty of the manslaughter of John Ward at Mr Nally's farmyard in Funshinaugh, Cross in Co Mayo on October 14, 2004.

For their service, Mr Justice Paul Carney rewarded the jury with the prospect of never again having to do jury duty.

For Padraic Nally, the ordeal was far from over. The Mayo farmer had been convicted of manslaughter and was released on bail to appear before Justice Paul Carney for sentencing in Dublin on November 11.

For Marie Ward and her children, the job of picking up the pieces and getting on with the rest of their lives was just beginning.

***

On the morning of Friday, November 11, Padraic Nally left his home in Funshinaugh, Cross in Co Mayo. Padraic had spent his whole life on his farm in Funshinaugh but that morning, he had no idea what was in store for him in Dublin. Padraic didn't know if he'd ever make it back home again and he wasn't sure if he would ever again get the chance to walk his land or see his animals in the fields.

That day in Dublin, Padraic Nally was sentenced to six years in prison for the manslaughter of John 'Frog' Ward. Addressing the court, Mr Justice Paul Carney said it was the most difficult matter he had to deal with in more than 14 years on the bench.

The judge accepted that Nally was initially protecting his property against an invasion from someone who was up to no good. It was events after this point that informed his sentencing.

Nally had no previous convictions and was considered at low risk of re-offending. Mr Justice Carney jailed him for six years.

John Ward's widow, Marie, and other Ward family members expressed disappointment at the jury verdict and the sentencing.

Meanwhile, Nally's legal team said they would be seeking leave to appeal, claiming the trial judge usurped the jury's function when he refused to allow them to consider a full defence argument of self-defence. If this defence had succeeded in July 2005, Nally would have walked free.

In reality, the saga was far from over.

Chapter 9
Thomas Murray's Brutal Murders

Thomas Murray from Ballygar in Co Galway was just 17 years old when he savagely killed Willie Mannion, an elderly neighbour, in 1981. It was the first of two brutal murders he would commit in his home community. Nineteen years later, while on temporary release from prison, Murray struck again. This time, 80-year-old Nancy Nolan was the unfortunate victim. A retired teacher in Ballygar, Nancy had taught the troubled youth during his school days.

Unlike other attacks on elderly people across rural Ireland, Thomas Murray had no desire to steal from Willie Mannion or Nancy Nolan when he arrived at their homes in 1981 and 2000 respectively. However, while monetary gain was not his objective, the crimes were similar to others in rural Ireland at the time insofar as they were random attacks on elderly and vulnerable people.

According to a Garda report to the Director of Public Prosecutions on October 5, 1981, Murray was not particularly bright and had come under adverse notice both at primary and secondary school. He only attended the latter for approximately one year and he was a 'strong suspect' for such things as puncturing his classmates' bicycles and prodding them in the classroom with a compass.

The report went on to note that Murray had taken a dislike to a female neighbour. He had sent obscene letters to her and was suspected of attempting to burn her car. He was charged in 1981 with unlawfully using language towards her, which calculated to cause a breach of the peace. However, the case was struck out when both parties agreed to shake hands.

Undoubtedly, Thomas Murray was an unusual character in the small and peaceful North Galway community. He was something of a loner growing up and had become a bit of a troublemaker throughout his childhood and adolescent years. Nonetheless, nobody could have predicted the cold-blooded killings that awaited the quiet town of Ballygar.

Willie Mannion was a 73-year-old bachelor farmer. Typical of the times he lived in, Willie's door was always open and the kettle was never far from the boil. Neighbours and friends would come and go and Willie would always have a welcome for visitors to his home.

On a sunny Sunday morning in July 1981, Willie encountered 17-year-old Thomas Murray after Mass in Ballygar. He was familiar with the Murrays, another local family in the area, and he shared a few words with the teenager outside the church that day. Thomas wouldn't have been the only person Willie spoke with after Mass. He was a popular and sociable farmer and there was nothing unusual about his fleeting conversation with Murray on the morning of July 19, 1981.

Hours later however, the disturbed and dangerous youth cycled to Willie Mannion's home, carrying a knife. When he entered the bachelor's home, he found Mannion sitting at the kitchen table. In a completely unprovoked attack, Murray stabbed him in the head more than a dozen times.

Retired Detective Garda Basil Johnson, who was part of a Divisional Investigation Unit in Roscommon-Galway East at the time, recalled the horrific murder and the utter disbelief in the community.

"Murray was only 17 when he attacked Willie Mannion in his own home for no apparent reason. The murder sent shockwaves through the close-knit community. When he made a statement eventually, his story was that he had met Willie Mannion at Mass that Sunday morning.

Murray had a perceived grievance that Willie made some comment about selling him bad hay or having a bad cow or something like that. In reality, the likelihood is that Willie said nothing of the sort.

That evening, Murray went to see Willie. He was a bachelor and lived in what they called a tighín at the time. It was a small prefab with a kitchen and a bedroom. Murray sat down and spoke with Willie for a few minutes and then all of a sudden, he got up from the table and stabbed him 19 or 20 times down on top of the head, neck and eyes. It was a most vicious attack," explained Mr Johnson.

After brutally killing the pensioner, Murray returned home and, as though nothing had happened, went to a local carnival that night. Willie's bloodied body was discovered the next day, slumped on a chair in his kitchen.

The Gardaí were familiar with Murray at the time, but just for minor offences.

"He had one brother who had special needs and was in a care home. Thomas lived with his mother and father in Cloonlyon, Ballygar. After the attack on Willie, Murray's blood-stained clothes had been burned at the family home. In the ashes from the range in the kitchen, we found the zip from his jacket and that was enough to follow it up. That time, of course, there was no power of arrest and there was very little that could be done with forensics so really, we needed a confession," added Mr Johnson.

Thomas Murray was first interviewed by Gardaí on July 28 but claimed innocence. The following day, he was admitted to hospital having being found unconscious in bed. According to the Garda report, it was clear he had taken a drug overdose, probably by means of tablets which were prescribed for his brother.

When the Gardaí eventually apprehended Murray, he was working in the family bog. "Thomas was walking back up towards the road with the donkey and cart carrying a load of turf and we were waiting for him. We invited him to the station because there was no power of arrest at the time. It was ironic really that we found him in the bog because 19 years later when he murdered Nancy Nolan, he hid the murder weapon – a lump hammer – in a bog hole right there."

At the station on September 2, 1981, Murray made a statement to the Gardaí. He admitted the crime but refused to disclose where he had hidden the weapon. It would appear that there was some element of premeditation in the murder as the knife used, according to his statement, had been taken from his kitchen at home a few days previously and hidden in a field. Later the same day, he told Gardaí he had planned the crime but 'not for too long' and insisted he would not do it again.

Murray's first court appearance was in Mountbellew in Co Galway and from here, he was remanded in custody to St Patrick's Institution on September 3, 1981. That day, the Gardaí were still out searching for the weapon but life was about to get a whole lot easier for the search party.

"Another detective and I were bringing Murray to St Pat's after the court. We were passing by the general area where he lived on the way to Dublin and Thomas said he'd like to go down past his home place. We had a huge search team out that day looking for the murder weapon so we sent word to them that we were passing that way and to make themselves scarce. Along the way, I asked Thomas if he'd like to tell us where the weapon was hidden. He was humming and hawing and then he pointed to a spot where he said he had thrown the knife. I rolled down the window and threw out a marker. We kept going but within 15 minutes, the search team had found the weapon," recalled the retired detective.

On the recommendation of the medical doctor at St Patrick's Institution, Murray was transferred to the Mater Hospital on November 5, 1981, for EEG treatment, which allows doctors to view and record changes in brain activity.

A liaison meeting on November 19 discussed the case of Thomas Murray, who it was said, had been in the care of the institution since November 5 but was no longer showing any signs of harming himself. He was described as emotionally immature with a surprisingly low level of intelligence and also as being borderline psychotic with some elements of schizophrenia. On December 14, the medical officer recommended Murray's transfer to the Central Mental Hospital.

On February 22, 1982, Thomas Murray was convicted of the murder of Willie Mannion and sentenced to life imprisonment. He had pleaded guilty but gave no evidence in court. Murray remained in the Central Mental Hospital until April 15, 1983, when he was taken to Mountjoy Prison. On March 7, 1984, his transfer to Arbour Hill Prison was ordered. On November 26, 1985, he was returned to Mountjoy.

Throughout his time in prison, he was assessed on numerous occasions and in May 1990, Murray's case was considered by the newly established Sentence Review Group.

Dr Hardiman – in a letter dated May 18, 1990 – noted that on occasions when Murray was admitted to the Central Mental Hospital, he was not considered to be suffering from a mental illness and that at a recent interview, there was no evidence of any such illness. In light of that, Dr Hardiman felt he had no particular recommendation or contribution to make but said it would be worthwhile for the Welfare Service to look into the family/community situation as this could have an important bearing on any possible release.

***

In 1992, Murray began to get parole – day release at first and then for longer periods. As per his parole conditions, Murray would sign on in the local Garda station once or twice a week and then, at the end of the month, he would return to prison. Provided he was behaving himself, the release order would be renewed.

When Thomas secured a job in Galway City, working on the buildings, it looked as though he was trying to turn his life around. In July 1998 however, he exposed himself to some women. His parole was immediately cancelled. He was convicted of indecent exposure and sent back to prison.

After a while, he started to get one-day releases again and his father, Tom, would take him out in the morning and return him to prison at night. At a meeting in Castlerea Prison on September 27, 1999, attended by the governor, assistant governor, a chief officer, a probation and welfare officer, and one officer from the Department, it was indicated that Thomas Murray would continue to get outings with the probation officer or the chaplain to visit his father. It was stated that he was greatly feared in the locality and that any overnight stay there would cause a panic. The meeting decided that if his father would collect and return him, Murray could get out on temporary release for one day every two weeks.

Between October 18, 1999, and February 14, 2000, Thomas Murray was granted temporary release on 20 occasions – for 19 of these releases, he was unaccompanied but was collected and returned by his father. While on day release in February 2000, Thomas Murray killed Nancy Nolan, a retired school teacher.

Nancy had taught Thomas in school and on February 14 that year, their paths crossed in a shop in Ballygar. Nancy was seen bidding him the time of day. Everybody else in Ballygar would shun Thomas because they were afraid of him but Nancy – always trying to see the best in people – nodded at him and said hello. Sadly, this simple and kind-hearted gesture would lead to her death.

What was most tragic about Nancy Nolan's death was that it was avoidable. The Gardaí who had worked on the Willie Mannion case had written reports advising that Murray never be released and warning that he would kill again. The parole board, however, decided he deserved another chance.

"Murray killed Nancy Nolan for no reason. It was a random attack on an elderly woman in the middle of the day. Nancy had been in town shopping and had gone home with some groceries. She wasn't long at home when a knock came to the door and it was Thomas. He pulled a lump hammer out and beat her to death in the hallway of her home. Then, he simply closed the door and walked away. Murray went back into prison as normal that night and Nancy's body was discovered a day or two later when a neighbour reported not seeing her in a few days. Murray was immediately the prime suspect and we had to build up a case," recalled Mr Johnson.

Murray was taken out of the prison one morning and questioned in relation to the death of the retired teacher but he made no admission, good, bad or indifferent. When some new evidence emerged, the Gardaí were given the authority to take him out of prison for a second time. Again, there was no admission. Murray didn't cooperate with the investigation at all. In fact, he wouldn't even speak to the Gardaí or answer any of their questions.

For some reason however, Thomas Murray felt he had built up something of a relationship with Detective Garda Johnson and the detective's decision to foster this 'relationship' eventually proved fruitful.

"I got on with him, for want of a better description, and once or twice he looked for me to go to see him so I went and visited him in prison. I think he really just wanted someone to talk to but he wouldn't discuss the murder at all. I kept hoping that at some stage he would."

The visits went on for several months and then finally came the breakthrough. "Eventually, I got a call one Bank Holiday weekend. It was late in the evening and I wasn't on duty but when I answered the phone and found the governor of Castlerea Prison on the other end of the line telling me that Murray wanted to see me urgently, I immediately stopped what I was doing and drove to Castlerea. I called Sergeant Tom Fitzmaurice (now a Garda inspector). He was off duty too but he was available and he came with me," explained the retired detective.

Murray was waiting in an interview room in Castlerea Prison when Detective Garda Johnson and Sergeant Fitzmaurice arrived. He made a full statement of admission.

"It wasn't as simple as getting a murder admission from Thomas that evening. We had to go through everything and had to make sure every detail was right in what he was telling us. Thomas said he saw her in town that day; told us he was using the father's car and where he parked the car; where Nancy Nolan's car was when he arrived; how long he was in the house; what he had done; and what happened next. It all had to be gone through meticulously, it wasn't as simple as just getting a confession out of him. We had to make sure it all made sense and fitted in with the timeline. It was time consuming, every little detail had to be covered, but we had to make sure he wasn't just admitting the murder for the sake of it."

Crucially, Murray also informed the Gardaí about the weapon.

"Up until this, we had no idea what he had used to kill Nancy Nolan but Murray told us he had used a lump hammer and said it was in a bog

Nancy Nolan, a retired school teacher, was found dead at her home near Ballygar, Co Galway. Thomas Murray was later convicted of the murder. Picture courtesy of Ray Ryan/Tuam Herald.

Thomas Murray Jnr of Cloonlyon, Ballygar, Co Galway is led inside Mountbellew District Court, charged with the murder of retired schoolteacher Nancy Nolan. Murray was convicted of the murder of Willie Mannion in Ballygar in 1981 and the murder of Nancy Nolan in Ballygar in 2000. Picture: Ray Ryan/Tuam Herald.

Legendary Mayo footballer Henry Dixon suffered two attacks by raiders at his pub in Claremorris in Co Mayo in the space of five days.
On January 9, 1995, the 76-year-old was hospitalised after raiders broke into his premises for a second time. Picture courtesy of Cormac Hanley

Michael Joseph Kelly of Castleblakney, Ballinasloe, Co Galway, pictured leaving the Court of Criminal Appeal in Dublin in January 2008. Mr Kelly sought to have his murder conviction quashed and claimed to be a victim of the miscarriage of justice. He was convicted in 1983 of the murder of Margaret Glynn at Keaves, Ballinamore Bridge, outside Ahascragh, Co Galway in 1981. Pic: Courtpix

Christy Hanley who was discovered dead in his home in Kilbeggan,
Co Westmeath May 22, 2008. Picture: James Flynn/APX.

The remains of Christy Hanley being removed from his home in
Kilbeggan, Co Westmeath on May 22, 2008.
Picture: James Flynn/APX.

Norfolk farmer Tony Martin shot and killed an intruder at his home in August 1999. He was initially jailed for life for the murder of 16-year-old Fred Barras. His murder conviction was later reduced to manslaughter. The case prompted national debate on the measures homeowners could take to protect themselves. Tony Martin's case was cited in the media in Ireland at various stages during the Padraic Nally trial. Picture: Eastern Daily Express

Padraic Nally of Funshinaugh, Cross in Co Mayo, was first convicted of the manslaughter of John Ward. During a retrial at Dublin's Four Courts, Nally was found not guilty. Picture: Peter Wilcock.

John 'Frog' Ward, who was shot dead at Padraic Nally's farm in Funshinaugh, Cross, Co Mayo, on October 14, 2004. Picture: Peter Wilcock.

Padraic Nally's country cottage at Funshinaugh, Cross in Mayo – the scene of the shooting of John Ward. Picture: Peter Wilcock

John Ward with son and a family friend. Picture: Peter Wilcock.

Marie Ward, the wife of the late John 'Frog' Ward, pictured with some of the couple's children during the initial trial in Castlebar in July 2005.
Picture: Peter Wilcock.

Marie Ward, wife of the late John Ward, and her son Tom who was with his father at the time of the shooting, arrive for the trial in Castlebar. Picture: Peter Wilcock.

A passer-by stops for a chat as Padraic Nally leads his supporters across the Mall in Castlebar during his trial in July 2005. Picture: Peter Wilcock.

Padraic Nally's only sister, Maureen, was by his side during the trial in Castlebar and again throughout the retrial at Dublin's Four Courts. Picture: Peter Wilcock.

In December 2006, following the not guilty verdict at Dublin's Four Courts, Padraic Nally comes home to his farm in Funshinaugh, Cross in Co Mayo. Picture: Henry Wills/Western People.

hole in the family's own bog. Nancy's glasses had been taken too and we asked him about that. He told us where they were in a particular wood in the area. The next day, the search team were sent out and within about an hour they had found the hammer. Later that evening, they located Nancy's glasses," explained Mr Johnson.

The brutal murders of Willie Mannion and Nancy Nolan were similar in that the victims had been taken unawares. With Willie Mannion, Murray had produced a knife from his pocket and stabbed him repeatedly. In the case of Nancy Nolan, she had opened the door to Murray and he pulled out a lump hammer and bludgeoned her to death. Nancy was a frail old woman in her 80s and like the murder of Willie Mannion, Murray had acted in a cowardly fashion.

"He had some kind of a weird fixation on killing and on blood and he wouldn't take on someone who could fight back. He was a coward and would only target the elderly and frail. He should never have been released from prison and he should never get out again," opined Mr Johnson.

In December 2000, 37-year-old Thomas Murray received a life sentence at the Central Criminal Court after he pleaded guilty to murdering Nancy Nolan on February 14 that year. Mrs Nolan's son and five daughters sat in the Central Criminal Court, trying to make sense of their mother's murder. After the sentencing, Mrs Nolan's brother questioned the unsupervised temporary release that Murray was enjoying when he carried out his second murder in less than 20 years.

***

In 2001, the then Justice Minister, John O'Donoghue, established an enquiry into the circumstances surrounding Murray's releases from prison, considering all of the evidence pointed to reasons why he should have remained behind bars. In the midst of the enquiry, it emerged that just over a year before Murray claimed his second victim, the governor of Castlerea Prison, Daniel Scannell, had warned that the Galway man would kill again.

Of course, Gardaí had opposed Murray's temporary release on a number of occasions, describing the prisoner as a person of extremely violent nature and opposing his release on the grounds it would constitute a threat to the community.

A major overhaul of the way life-term prisoners are managed was ordered after the independent report – commissioned by the Department of Justice – showed up weaknesses in the system. The report called for a tightening of procedures and a general review of the temporary release of inmates who committed violent crimes.

During the enquiry, Governor Scannell said his comment to the local review meeting in late 1998, in relation to Murray killing again, had to be taken in context. Mr Scannell pointed out that after a lengthy process of engagement with the probation and welfare officer, these concerns were reduced.

Former Secretary General of the Department of the Gaeltacht, John Olden, was commissioned to carry out the report and noted that Gardaí were generally critical of decisions to release prisoners who had committed serious crimes.

On March 14, 1995, the then Justice Minister, Mrs Nora Owen, first approved fortnightly renewable temporary release for Murray, subject to strict reporting and curfew restrictions. The subsequent significant decisions – his return to prison in September 1996 for reasons of reported breaches of conditions; the renewal of his temporary release programme in April 1997; his return to prison following charges relating to indecent exposure; his continued detention following completion of the sentence imposed for that offence; and his slow progress through the penal system to occasional temporary releases – were not referred back to the Minister of the day.

On resumption of his life sentence, following reports of the indecent exposure incident in July 1998, Murray received no further temporary release until the completion of his six-month sentence for this offence.

A subsequent series of accompanied temporary releases, of a few hours duration each, were approved by a senior Department official in January 1999 for compassionate humanitarian reasons; to visit his critically ill mother in hospital. Murray received two temporary releases on January 27 and 28, 1999, to attend the removal and burial of his mother in the company of a probation and welfare officer. A series of monthly temporary releases to his father, accompanied by either the chaplain or a probation and welfare officer, was then approved by the same senior Department official. These began in late February 1999 and continued up to the middle of October that year.

The Olden Report also confirmed that Murray had 73 sessions with the probation and welfare officer in Castlerea in a 19-month period up to February 2000. These meetings showed that Murray had a difficult personality and would need a lot of attention before he could be released safely into the community. The report noted that Thomas Murray was not mentally ill but socially inadequate and on his record as a prisoner, he would not have been regarded as likely to commit a violent attack while on temporary release.

A memo from the jail's probation and welfare officer, dated six months before Nancy Nolan's murder, said Murray's thinking was 'highly distorted in his personal relationships and that the vindictive and petty side of him frequently seen in prison is tied directly to his offending'.

Mr Olden said he found it disturbing to find differing accounts of a meeting where it was decided to allow Murray out on temporary release to visit his father without a probation officer. It was on one of these visits he murdered Nancy Nolan.

The Olden Report recommended a tightening up on procedures for managing life-sentence prisoners but added that it would be a real mistake to take no risk in the future as the vast majority of people sentenced to life imprisonment did not seriously re-offend after release. It added that Mr Scannell's comments that Murray would "kill again" did not mean the governor or anyone else in the prison service felt that significant risk would arise on occasional releases.

In addition to the two brutal murders of Willie Mannion and Nancy Nolan in Ballygar, Thomas Murray was a suspect in the murder of taxi driver Eileen Costello O'Shaughnessy, at Tinkers Lane, approximately eight miles from Galway city, on November 30, 1997.

"Thomas was on release when Eileen Shaughnessy was murdered and I was in Galway working on the investigation. Murray came up as a suspect and right up until the day I retired in 2002, I visited him in prison to see if he would confess but he never made any admission. I think he still has it in his head that he'll get out some time and if he did kill her and admitted it, this would be the final nail in the coffin. I don't believe he should ever be released," opined retired Detective Garda Johnson.

The mother-of-two was viciously beaten to a pulp after she innocently transported her murderer to a quiet, isolated laneway in Claregalway on the cold winter's night. Her lifeless body was then dragged further along the muddy pathway and dumped near a gate. The following morning, a local farmer made the grisly discovery.

Nobody has ever been prosecuted for Ms O'Shaughnessy's death.

Ironically, in April 2008, Thomas Murray's elderly father was viciously assaulted and robbed when three people broke into his house at Cloonlyon, about three miles from Ballygar on the Galway-Roscommon border.

75-year-old, Tommy Murray was subjected to a vicious assault when two men and a woman broke into his home. The raiders escaped with what was described as a substantial amount of cash.

Tommy Murray told Gardaí that the break-in occurred shortly before 10pm on Monday night, April 14. Mr Murray's hands and legs were tied by the raiders and he was beaten around the head as they ransacked the house looking for cash and valuables.

When the thieves fled, Mr Murray was left lying on the floor. Half-an-hour later, the pensioner managed to free himself and made his way to a neighbour's house, where he raised the alarm.

Chapter 10
Life Behind Bars for Nally

On November 11, 2005, Padraic Nally was sentenced to six years in prison for the manslaughter of John 'Frog' Ward at Nally's farmyard in Funshinaugh, Cross, Co Mayo. The conviction was recorded on July 20 that year at the Central Criminal Court, sitting in Castlebar. He was remanded on continuing bail pending his sentencing in Dublin.

Up until this point, Padraic Nally's life was largely spent walking the fields of his farm in South Mayo. A bachelor farmer, living alone, Padraic knew every inch of his land. Farming was his whole life. He was comfortable in his own company and Padraic was most content when he was spending time amongst his animals.

Life as he knew it was about to change and the confinement and solitude of prison life was to become his new reality. Leaving home to travel to Dublin on Friday, November 11, Padraic knew his fate was sealed. While the Ward family were adamant that Nally should have been given a longer period behind bars, the Mayo farmer was shocked when the six-year sentence was announced in Dublin.

"I was convicted in July and then when I was sentenced in November, it was a big shock to me that I got so long for protecting my property and my home. I had been burgled so often and that didn't seem to be taken into consideration. When I got out of bed, at home, on the morning of the sentencing, I was saying to myself that I might not be back here for years again, to sleep in my own bed, spend time in my own home, to look after my livestock and to see my family, friends and neighbours. It was hard knowing that I was facing a sentence and looking at being away from home for the first time really," he recalled.

Before he left Funshinaugh, he took one last walk around the farm.

"I went out to the fields and sort of said goodbye to the animals. I didn't know if this was the last time I'd see them or not. Apart from that though, I wasn't really worried about my livestock that morning, I was just afraid of what would happen in court that day."

Nally was first taken to Mountjoy, before being moved on Sunday morning to the Midlands Prison in Portlaoise. Life behind bars was a huge shock to the system for the Mayo farmer but he knew he had no choice but to adjust.

"Going to prison was all very strange. There was the fear of other prisoners because you didn't know the situation you were in. Walking around the yard, you were all the time looking over your shoulder, especially in the evening when it was dark. You didn't see anyone or know anyone that was coming up behind you. I was in a single cell. One of the prisoners in the cell beside me was from Mayo and there was another Mayo man across the landing. It took me a while to get to know the prisoners but I got to know some of them over the Christmas," he explained.

"A lot of them came to me and identified themselves. They knew who I was because it was such a high profile case for a long time. They all said to me that I shouldn't be in there, when all I was trying to do was defend my house and my property. I got on well with everybody and I didn't interfere with anybody's business, I just got on with doing my daily work. The prison officers were good to me too," he continued.

As Nally was being transported to Portlaoise Prison, the prison officers were listening to Marian Finucane on the radio.

"There was some guy on the radio with her and he was 'Nally this and Nally that'. I was browned off with the whole lot of it. He was saying they should put me in a cell, lock it and let me rot in there. I was really vexed.

"Some of the papers said awful stuff about me too, talked a lot of shit about me. You have to weigh it all up though, I suppose I wasn't used to dealing with the media and then, all of a sudden, everyone wanted to talk to me. Some were looking to make a fool out of me," he opined.

Prison life took a lot of getting used to for Padraic. Even a simple thing like making a phone call wasn't straight forward anymore.

"You couldn't just walk up to the phone and make a call. There'd be a queue and then you'd only be allowed on the phone for a couple of minutes. It wasn't as simple as dialling the number either. You were given a code and when you went to dial out, you'd have to give that code and then they'd dial the number you wanted. It wasn't straight forward. A lot of people were wondering why I wasn't phoning them but I didn't know what to do.

"One guy came to help me, to show me what to do but then he got frustrated. He threw down the phone and left me there. This other fellow came over to me then. He was a farmer too. He showed me what to do; he knew the ins and outs of the phone. I'm still in contact with him," Padraic explained.

"There was one fellow one day and he couldn't get through to his family. He was so frustrated and mad that he hit the phone against the wall. I went up to him and told him to calm down. I said to him that if he was seen acting like that, they might take the phone off him entirely for the week. He came to me later and apologised. He had been upset. He was in court that day and was turned down in his appeal," he recalled.

During his 11 months behind bars, Padraic spent time in a number of different prisons but, according to the Mayo man, 'they're all the same really'.

"It was the same set-up no matter where you were. There was a big hall where we'd go for breakfast. We were only allowed wear trousers and a shirt; your shoes and belt had to be left outside the door. You got given a pair of trousers and they could be like a barrel. You'd go with your tray and plate for your breakfast and you'd get a pot of tea, so you'd have a pot of tea on a tray and you'd be trying to hold up your trousers with one hand and carry the tray with the other.

"One of my first days in prison, there were a heap of prison officers in the breakfast room. As I was walking towards one of them, he asked me: 'are you alright now?' 'I'd be a damn sight better if I had a belt to put on my trousers,' I told him. They were all looking at me laughing, they had no idea I was going to say that."

Padraic had no complaints about the food in prison. For breakfast there'd be apples, pears and bananas, then Rice Krispies or Cornflakes too. Each prisoner had their own teapot and cup and at dinner time, they were handed a plate with their meal – beef, pork or lamb. At each meal time, prisoners would be given teabags, bread and butter. At 4pm, there would be another snack, sometimes sausages with bread or toast. There was no shortage of food during Padraic's time in prison and he never went hungry.

On the inside, the day began at 8am, when the cells would be opened and the prisoners would line up for breakfast, before taking their food back to their cell. Always an early riser on the farm, Padraic would often be out of bed by 6am but he couldn't leave the cell for another two hours. When he and his fellow inmates would collect their breakfast and return to their cells, the locks would be closed again. At 8.30am, the cell doors would be opened and prisoners would sweep and mop their cells and leave out the laundry.

Throughout his 11 months in prison, Padraic always worked in the gardens.

"I was asked to go out in the garden after the first week and I went out. I was happy doing it but I didn't have a choice anyway. There wasn't much going on at that particular time, the plants had been sewn earlier in the year, so it was just covering the plants, protecting them from the weather conditions. There'd be other odd jobs then for the run of the day in the garden. The air wasn't too fresh and in the wintertime, it was damp and breezy. We were given overalls and shoes and a cap by the prison to do the work. We were out regardless of the weather."

Padraic wasn't always popular with the other prisoners in the garden, probably because he was constantly anxious to work and keep busy.

"Some of them were afraid I'd show them up, but I put up with it. Work in the garden involved cutting lawns, sewing plants, transplanting plants and watering the garden. There was a vegetable plot but it was educational more than anything. Rhubarb, strawberries, vegetable marrow, potatoes, carrots, parsnips, lettuce and cabbage plants were all sewn from seed. Then there was a big turnout of flowers. There were flower boxes outside the prison and the same way inside. There were flowers in tunnels, on the landings and in the governor's office. All sorts of flowers, plants and shrubs were sewn and the prisoners in the garden were shown how to sew them and look after them," he explained.

For Padraic and his fellow prisoners in the garden, work was from 9am until 12 noon, when they were called back into the prison for dinner. "We used to go back inside, back to our cells to collect our trays and then we'd go to get our dinner. Like at breakfast time, we'd take our trays back to the cell to eat. At 2pm, we'd go back out and report to the garden for duty."

For those who weren't working in the garden or elsewhere in the prison, there was a choice of going to the recreation yard or to the fitness room in the morning and afternoon. "Some of them would wait in the cell and more of them would go to the yard. The cell doors would be left open so prisoners could go out to the yard for fresh air. Some of them never left the cell, they wouldn't go out at all," he said.

After dinner, work continued in the garden until 4pm, or sometimes a little earlier. "The prison officers would sometimes give us a rest at 3.30pm and sometimes not. I always kept working away regardless. I'd have a bucket of weeds pulled while some would be playing cards or drinking cups of tea, but it didn't bother me what anyone else was doing, I was happy to be out working in the garden."

The prisoners would return to their cells at 4pm for a snack and then at 5.30pm, everybody was allowed out to the yard for a walk.

"You could make a phone call at that stage of the day. That was the best time because people, on the outside, would be out at work all day. If you tried to ring earlier and even if you didn't get through, you could lose your phone call for the evening."

At 7pm, the prisoners were called back to the landing, where the medics would be available for anyone who wanted them. At 8pm, the cells were locked for the night.

During his time in prison, Padraic found it particularly difficult to be confined to his cell between 12 noon and 2pm – a time when he would normally have been incredibly busy back at home in Funshinaugh.

"When I was out in the garden, at least I could be walking around. Inside in the cell, my attitude was always different. I had too much time to concentrate and think about what was going on. During that time, I'd always be thinking about home. That would be one of the busiest times of the day on the farm and I certainly wouldn't be sitting down for two hours. I found that very hard to take," he said.

Padraic's first visitor to the prison was his sister Maureen. Some of his neighbours also came to visit during the first week.

"A lot of my neighbours visited me during my time there. You were allowed eight visitors a month and you had to nominate the people who were coming in to see you. As a rule you'd only have the one visit in the month from the same person. But as well as Maureen coming to visit, I had regular visits from Paddy Rock, Mike Varley, Andy Lavin, Tom Halloran, Paddy McTigue, Martin Mellette and a lot more then throughout the country. They came from various parts of the country; from Cork, Galway, Dundalk and Laois to see me."

While it was great for Padraic to see familiar faces during his time in prison, watching his visitors walk out the door and knowing he couldn't go home with them was sometimes very difficult.

"I was at a loss to see them moving back out to their freedom and me having to go back to my cell again. When we went to Mass on a Sunday morning in prison, the Mass Leaflet said 'Behind The Door' in big letters on the front and all the time I was in there, I thought of that. That was how it was and I just had to get used to not having my freedom."

Sunday mornings started the same as all others.

"We'd start the day by cleaning out our cells and then get ready for Mass. Some people dressed very well for Mass, they had clothes with them for that day. But it was an ordinary day really, except that you took in Mass. There was a 20ft high wall around the prison and we used to go up three stories to Mass on a Sunday. Even all the way up there, you still couldn't see out over the wall. You'd see a few chimneys in the distance, that's all. After Mass, we went out to the yard for an hour and then at 11.30am, we could go to the library for books. I didn't do much reading inside, except for the daily papers."

Similarly, Christmas Day 2005 was just like any other day for Padraic.

"It was a lonely spot to spend Christmas and December 25 was just like any other ordinary day in the prison, except that there was turkey and ham for dinner. There was supposed to be rashers in the morning too, but I don't really recall whether the rashers were available or not. It was like any other day, only lonelier, because I was away from home and missed being there and being with my family and friends."

It was nerve-wrecking for Padraic at times in prison, not being able to be out on the land at home to see what was happening. Thankfully though, he was exceptionally lucky to have wonderful friends and neighbours on the outside, who continued to manage and run his farm while he was behind bars.

"My neighbours were brilliant. There were four or five in particular who really looked after everything to the best of their ability in my absence. They all had their own farms to look after and it was a lot to expect them to look after mine as well, but they did a great job. There was someone there every day and they did the best they could over a long period of time. I was giving directions from inside to make sure everything was being looked after. Without the support from friends and neighbours, I wouldn't have been able to hold on to my livestock. I knew that the neighbours were looking after everything but it was strange not to know what a new calf looked like or what sort of a calf the cow had. It was hard to have missed all that," he noted.

In prison, Padraic soon learned how to behave around the other prisoners.

"I was used to talking to people on the farm or at marts throughout my life. I got to know a lot of people in a short time in prison through conversation, but you didn't ask them any questions or personal details. You just had to get on with your life in there. It can be rough and tumble in prison, some people can be fine but you have to know who you're dealing with and be able to judge them," he pointed out.

While Nally counted the days to his release, others had very different ideas and some of his fellow prisoners were intent on scaring him.

"One guy told me I wouldn't last three days after I got out until they'd have me killed. I heard another guy one day say: 'who'd want to leave here? The money has changed twice since I've been in and I won't know what it looks like when I get out. I'll be lost when I leave here.' The way he saw it, he was in prison with a roof over his head, a bed to sleep in every night, electricity, water, heating and enough food to eat. I wasn't thinking like that at all. I wanted to get out and get home to my farm."

As well as the support of Padraic's family and friends, there were so many others who sent messages to the Mayo farmer while he was in jail.

Padraic received more than 2,000 cards, letters and messages to his prison cell and the letters didn't just come from Ireland. Envelopes were arriving every day from all over the world; from New Zealand, Australia, China, South Africa, Portugal, Dubai, Taiwan, the Holy Land, Fatima and lots of other places besides.

"There were a lot of messages and letters, where people were telling me that they were in similar situations to myself. Some of them were beaten up by intruders and in one particular instance, I got a letter from a relative of a man who followed intruders from his home and got a massive heart attack and died on the spot. It was a big shock to me to think that such a thing would happen and that there were so many people around the country living in such fear for so long. Several sent me letters about different versions of raids and about being abused on streets. I didn't think it was going on to such a large scale. Somebody else sent me a letter saying that they had been home from America to visit relations and they were tied up in their own home. Others sent me lovely letters offering support and telling me they were praying for me. It was somewhat comforting," he said.

Before Padraic left prison, he managed to avoid a common prison ritual.

"There are a few things that normally happen when you're leaving prison. I didn't know about them until I was jailed. There's a television in every cell in prison and when prisoners are leaving, they often throw water over the television set. That's a personal choice, it's something prisoners do but I certainly didn't do it before I left," he explained.

The second ritual, on the other hand, is not a choice.

"They call it the 'baptism' – it's when water is thrown on you the evening before you leave. When you're on the landing the night before you go home, the prisoners gather around you and throw jugs of water at you. I don't know what the women do but that's what happens among the men in prison. I saw several of these 'baptisms', where they would crowd around the prisoner and a few of them would hold him and the others would throw water in his face. It was a ritual but I managed to get away without that happening."

Chapter 11
Murders in Ahascragh

When an elderly brother and sister perished in a house fire at their home in Ahascragh in Co Galway in 1981, it seemed like a tragic accident. The bodies of 85-year-old Martin and 87-year-old Margaret Glynn were discovered at their home at Keaves, Ballinamore Bridge, outside Ahascragh in Co Galway on Sunday, November 15, 1981. The fire started at around 9.30am on the cold November morning and when neighbours saw flames emanating from the house, local men Michael Donohue and Michael Kelly battled the blaze and tried to rescue the siblings. The men fought to reach the bedrooms of Martin and Margaret but their efforts were hampered by dense smoke.

The tragic deaths shocked and saddened friends and neighbours locally but when the initial results from the post mortem on Margaret's body proved inconclusive, the plot thickened for the investigating Gardaí.

The Murder Squad were called to assist with the investigation while Gardaí awaited further findings from the post mortems, carried out by the then State Pathologist, Dr John Harbison. Detectives from the Garda Technical Bureau were also enlisted to comb the house after the double tragedy shook the small tight-knit community.

What transpired from the investigations was that Margaret – or Maggie as she was known – was already dead when the fire broke out at the home she shared with her bachelor brother.

Retired Detective Garda Basil Johnson was involved with the investigation and recalled what transpired as Gardaí began to dig deeper.

"Michael Kelly used to do jobs around the house for Maggie and Martin and she had promised him she'd leave him the farm and whatever money they had when she died. Apparently Michael had found out the farm wasn't being left to him after all and he had a row with her in her room. Things got heated and he strangled her in the bed. It was an old farm house and Maggie always kept a candle by her bedside. To cover his tracks, he set fire to the bed with her in it, hoping nobody would be any the wiser. She was burned in her bed and initially it was treated as a terrible accident," explained Mr Johnson.

"The local Garda in Ahascragh had a suspicion that things weren't right. He'd have known the story and word had gotten around that Maggie had reneged on her promise to Michael Kelly. Michael used to do odd jobs around the house, bring them for their pension, that sort of thing. There was no family connection that I can remember.

"The post mortem showed that Maggie had been dead before the fire started. There was no smoke in her lungs and then it was discovered she had been strangled. Her bedroom was the only room that was really damaged by the fire. It was a small cottage. There was just a kitchen with a bedroom on either side. When we went to the other bedroom, we found her brother was dead in his bed. The post mortem found Martin had died of natural causes," added the retired detective.

Michael Kelly was subsequently arrested. This was the same Michael Kelly who had allegedly been shocked when he saw flames coming from the Glynn's home and had tried to rescue the elderly siblings.

"He made some admissions but not a lot. He was talking about a crutch that he had broken. He said he had words with her and in temper, threatened her with a crutch and broke it. Asked where it was, he said he had hidden it behind the dresser. There was a big old-fashioned dresser in her bedroom and I remember we went to the house and found the crutch. It was corroborative evidence," he recalled.

"Eventually, he did admit he choked her but said he didn't mean to do it. Apparently she had said to him 'don't kill me Michaleen, I'll give you the farm'. There wasn't a theft as such, it was all about the farm. But at the same time, it was much like other crimes where elderly people were attacked in their homes – at the end of the day, he wanted what wasn't his, regardless of whether it had been promised to him or not," continued Mr Johnson.

At a special sitting of Ballinasloe District Court on Monday, November 23, Michael Joseph Kelly, with addresses at Castleblakeney and at Keave, Ballinamore Bridge, was charged with the murder of Margaret Glynn. He was further charged with maliciously setting fire to a dwelling, knowing that Margaret Glynn was therein at the time.

At the Central Criminal Court in Dublin in March 1983, Michael Kelly pleaded not guilty to the murder of Margaret Glynn. He also denied the arson attack on Margaret Glynn's home.

The court heard Kelly had been trying to get into the house the evening before their deaths. He was the son of an old friend of the elderly pair and had come to live with them in January 1981 to help around the house and to assist with the care of Martin, who was bedridden.

The relationship had been amicable for some months and there was an understanding that the Glynns would leave their 12-acre holding to Michael. Things turned unpleasant when Maggie Glynn became difficult to please. On Saturday, November 14, the situation reached a peak when Kelly was locked out of the house. Eventually, at 3am, he had to put his shoulder to the door to get inside. The following morning, a fire engulfed the house.

On the third day of the hearing at the Central Criminal Court, the court heard Kelly had told detectives the reason he killed Maggie Glynn was 'because she had driven [him] insane, giving out and saying bad things about [him]'. He had made a statement to Gardaí, admitting he put a blanket over her face as she slept and pressed her neck with his hand until she stopped breathing. Kelly said he then lifted the blanket off her head, held it over a candle until it caught fire and threw the burning blanket onto the bed.

Giving evidence in court however, Mr Kelly's story was in total contrast to his statement. "I did not kill Maggie Glynn. I did not set fire to the house. The statement I made to detectives, I made it through fear. Suggestions that were made to me, I signed my name through fear," he told the court.

Kelly, then 29 years of age, was jailed for life when the jury found him guilty of murdering the 87-year-old spinster. He served 10 years in prison before being released.

Since being convicted of the murder of Maggie Glynn, Michael Kelly has continued to protest his innocence, claiming he has been the victim of a miscarriage of justice. In November 2007, Michael Kelly took his case to the Court of Criminal Appeal, arguing that the original prosecution case was flawed. He claimed his statement was made under duress and also attempted to discredit much of scientific, medical and technical evidence which led to the guilty verdict.

The case was adjourned to January 2008 and again, the Court of Criminal Appeal reserved judgement in the appeal. In May 2009, Michael Kelly failed in his effort to bring his appeal to the Supreme Court after the Court of Criminal Appeal rejected his arguments. The court, with Mr Justice Nicholas Kearns presiding – sitting with Mr Justice Michael Hanna and Mr Justice Patrick McCarthy – ruled that after careful consideration, they were satisfied that no law of public importance had been raised in Mr Kelly's application. The court found it would be inappropriate to allow the matter to go before the Supreme Court and said Mr Kelly's application was misconceived.

Mr Kelly continues to protest his innocence.

* * *

In 1993, the quiet village of Ahascragh was shocked to its very core once more when 59-year-old Bridget Flynn was found dead in her bed. Bridget had moved to Ahascragh a few years earlier from the family holding at Eskermore. Ironically, her move to a new county council cottage in Ahascragh was prompted by her growing fear of isolation. She, like so many others at the time, had become conscious of the dangers of living on her own in the countryside. She uprooted her life and moved to Ahascragh for security reasons and to be closer to the shops. Her decision reflected a growing concern among elderly people in rural Ireland at the time.

Bridget was living in as estate known as New Houses, occupied predominantly by an elderly community. She was a woman of simple routine. A regular Mass-goer at St Cuan's Church in Ahascragh, she would either walk or cycle to the Church each day. In the village, she would do her weekly shopping and loved to meet and talk to the locals. She was a frail lady and was described by friends at the time as 'a most inoffensive woman'.

On February 13 that year, Bridget's bludgeoned body was discovered in her home after neighbours reported seeing a window broken at the rear of the property. Bridget had not been seen since Friday morning and suspicions were raised locally when she failed to attend Mass at St Cuan's on Friday evening.

Detective Garda Basil Johnson was involved in the investigation of the case.

"Bridget was a quiet unassuming lady. She lived on her own and never did anything to offend anybody. Then one day, for no apparent reason, Willie Boden broke into her home to rob her. He found Bridget in her bed and there were suggestions that he tried to sexually assault her, the poor woman. He was only a young fella, she was a frail old lady," he recalled.

"He killed her – strangled her – but he lost his wallet on the bed. It must have fallen out of his pocket but it wasn't found straight away. There had been another suspect at the time, who was flying close to the wind but when the wallet was found during a second search at the house, the focus quickly changed to Willie Boden. He was a young man who was originally from between Ahascragh and Ballinasloe. It turned out it was Willie who had killed her. One day, as he was coming from the bog, we met him and he volunteered to come and help us with our enquiries. In the beginning, he tried to say somebody else had taken his wallet but eventually, he admitted killing her," explained Mr Johnson.

Continuing, the retired detective noted that the area known as New Houses in Ahascragh was a little estate of houses, mainly occupied by elderly residents.

"It was an opportunistic crime. Bridget was an elderly woman and wouldn't have been spending much. He broke in to see if there was any money in the house. He'd have known she was there but I don't think he knew her personally. It was a cowardly act."

On the morning of February 13, 1993, when neighbours reported that the kitchen window of her semi-detached bungalow had been broken, Gardaí forced their way into the house and found Bridget's lifeless body on the floor of her bedroom. She was wearing just her nightdress and had been badly beaten. She was pronounced dead at the scene.

William Thomas Boden of 14 New Houses, Ahascragh, was charged at a special sitting of Ballinasloe District Court the following Tuesday evening and remanded in custody to Banagher District Court on Tuesday, February 23. The following November, Boden pleaded guilty to Bridget Flynn's murder at the Central Criminal Court in Dublin.

In September 1994, the inquest into her death heard Bridget Flynn died from asphyxia resulting from the pressure of a boot or other hard object on the neck. The inquest also heard that the woman had been subjected to a brutal assault, apart from the injuries which caused her death.

Garda Brian Courcy told in inquest that he entered the dead woman's house on February 13, 1993, with Brendan O'Brien of Sonnagh, Ahascragh. Seconds later, he heard Mr O'Brien scream: "Oh Jesus Christ, who did this?"

Miss Flynn's body had a lot of blood on the face and head. She was dressed in a blue nightdress which was pulled up over her hips. There was a lot of blood on the sheets and pillow, as well as on the carpet.

Bridget Flynn's death was described at her Funeral Mass as being like a 'blackout' to the parish. In a random and evil act of violence and greed, her life had come to a tragic and abrupt end.

Chapter 12
Retrial Granted in Nally Case

Mayo farmer Padraic Nally had served 11 months in prison by the time his appeal was heard before the Court of Criminal Appeal in Dublin. In July 2005, a jury of five men and seven women – sitting in Castlebar – had found him not guilty of murder, but guilty of the manslaughter of John 'Frog' Ward.

On November 11 that year, the Mayo farmer was sentenced to six years in prison for the manslaughter of John Ward at Nally's home in Funshinaugh, Cross in Co Mayo on October 14, 2004. However, the circumstances surrounding the verdict had been met with varying degrees of criticism in the months that followed the sentencing.

Mr Nally's trial made history in July 2005, when the Central Criminal Court sat in Castlebar for the first time since the foundation of the State. After a six-day trial, Mr Justice Paul Carney, who presided over the case, told the jury that the option of acquittal was not open to them, stating that the amount of force used by Padraic Nally could not be objectively justified.

The esteemed judge made the order at the request of the prosecution, who argued that to allow the defence of self-defence to go to the jury would be to open the door to some form of 'prophylactic (preventative) killing as part of the legal regime of self-defence'. Mr Justice Paul Carney directed the jury that they could not acquit Mr Nally of the killing of John Ward, offering them just two options – they could find him guilty of murder or they could find him guilty of manslaughter. The one thing they could not do was set him free. After just two hours and 10 minutes of deliberations, the 12-person jury found Mr Nally guilty of manslaughter and he was subsequently sentenced to six years in prison.

The defence team was outraged at the judge's ruling and applied to the Court of Criminal Appeal to have the decision overturned. They were given leave to appeal.

During the appeal hearing, Mr Grehan, Senior Counsel for the defence, submitted that the single point of appeal against Padraic Nally's conviction was a very important constitutional point. He questioned whether or not there are any circumstances in which a trial judge could ever direct a jury that they must convict, in the absence of a concession by the defence that acquittal was not an option. Mr Grehan noted that in this case, the trial judge had done so at the request of the prosecution.

In their 18-page judgement, the three judges at the Court of Criminal Appeal – Mr Justice Nicholas Kearns, Mr Justice Diarmuid O'Donovan and Mr Justice Eamon de Valera – said Nally's defence at the trial had been one of self-defence.

At the conclusion of the case there was 'a rather unusual development' when Mr Paul O'Higgins, Senior Counsel for the prosecution, invited the trial judge to direct that the defence of self-defence should be allowed to go to the jury 'in a truncated form, shorn of any possibility that the jury might acquit altogether, on the basis that the amount of force used was so excessive as to destroy any notion that it was objectively reasonable and that in such circumstances it should only be open to the jury to convict of either murder or manslaughter'.

The Court of Criminal Appeal said that Mr O'Higgins had urged that the trial judge should not leave open the possibility that the jury might bring a complete acquittal which would 'be plainly perverse'. The court noted that the Supreme Court had held in the Davis case that the constitutional right to trial with a jury had, as a fundamental and absolutely essential characteristic, the right of a jury to deliver a verdict.

The Supreme Court had also held that while a trial judge has a right to direct a jury to enter a not guilty verdict, there was no corresponding right to direct a jury to enter a guilty verdict. The court had also reviewed several English cases concerning the role of trial judges and juries and their responsibilities.

The Appeal Court noted that unfortunately neither the Supreme Court decision in the Davis case nor any of the English authorities were opened to the trial judge in the Padraic Nally case.

"Perhaps this was because the proceedings were held procul ab urbe (far from the city) in circumstances where the marshalling of written legal authorities may have posed certain practical difficulties. Nonetheless, the prosecution should have anticipated that the nature of the ruling being sought was one which required support, if it was available, from decided authority. Quite clearly, the issue of self-defence was a central issue at every stage of this case."

The Court of Criminal Appeal went on to state that the judges had little doubt that, had the prosecution allowed this trial to proceed in the usual manner, the learned trial judge would have given appropriate directions to the jury in the usual form. They added that the usual form would have enabled the trial judge to express his opinion that the amount of force used could not, in his view, be objectively justified in the context of self-defence, but would have left the ultimate decision on that issue to the jury.

"As events transpired, the jury were denied the opportunity to return a verdict of not guilty, even if such a verdict may have flown in the face of the evidence and however inappropriate the learned trial judge may have considered such an outcome to be. The authorities, both in this and the neighbouring jurisdiction, make it abundantly clear however that the jurors, who swear an oath to deliver a verdict in accordance with the evidence, must retain the ultimate power to determine issues of guilt or innocence," the court heard.

"That must, of necessity, include the power to return a verdict which conflicts with the opinion of the learned trial judge, however experienced that judge may be. The question of whether the amount of force used is objectively reasonable is quintessentially a matter of fact for a jury."

The court also said that it wished to emphasise the important responsibility resting with counsel to place all relevant authorities before the trial judge when seeking rulings or directions in the course of a criminal trial.

In a nutshell, in a dramatic twist to one of the most socially divisive trials in modern Irish legal history, the Court of Criminal Appeal quashed Nally's conviction and ordered a retrial. The court ruled that the jury at Nally's trial should have been allowed to consider the full defence of self-defence and that it was a matter for the jury to decide whether the force used by Nally was reasonable and to return an acquittal.

Mr Justice Nicholas Kearns, presiding, said Nally should be admitted to bail on the same terms as before his trial, pending a retrial. After the three-minute hearing, Nally consulted with his lawyers, Mr Brendan Grehan, Senior Counsel, and Mr Michael Bowman, Barrister of Law – together with members of his family – before he was escorted by prison officers from the court. Mr Nally was then taken to the Midlands Prison to sign a bail bond before his release.

On his release, Nally did not return home to his Cross farm immediately, choosing to spend a short period away. However, a few days later, he was back in his rural dwelling, delighted to find that his farm had been expertly maintained by friends, neighbours and supporters in his absence.

Reports in the national media that weekend suggested that Mr Nally had been contacted by Englishman Tony Martin since his release from prison. Mr Martin had served a three-year sentence some years earlier after being jailed for the shooting of teenager Fred Barras, after he broke into Martin's farmhouse in 1999.

It had been stated in the national media that Tony had invited Padraic to come and stay with him in England if he wanted to lie low, offering him personal security advice. In addition, it was claimed that Mr Martin had warned the Mayo farmer he would need constant monitoring by the Gardaí and would need to wire his house with top-of-the-range security measures to stop any revenge attacks.

The reality of the situation, however, is that Padraic Nally has never had a conversation with Mr Martin, despite both men knowing of each other's existence. Meanwhile, some other reports at the time suggested the Gardaí were keeping a very close eye on Mr Nally and his farmyard as a means of protection following his release from prison. But, the Garda Press Office would not confirm or deny if this was the case, pointing out that it is their policy not to comment on the security arrangements in any individual case.

The reaction to the release from prison of the Cross farmer, Padraic Nally, was predictably emotional and straight away, looked set to be the precursor to another divisive debate in Irish society over the right to protect one's private property from intruders.

Following Padraic Nally's release – pending the retrial – the Mayo Traveller Support Group issued a statement, expressing their concern at the decision to quash Mr Nally's conviction. The group opined that the period surrounding the trial brought out much of the worst racist sentiment among some members of the settled community towards Travellers and said it had increased tension between the two communities.

Mr Ward's widow, Marie, chose not to comment or accept any invitation for media interviews following the Appeal Court's decision, but family members said they were 'very traumatised' by the ruling. By then, the 42-year-old mother-of-11 had left the Carrowbrowne Halting Site on the Headford Road in Galway, where she and her family had been living prior to John's death.

Of course, it is important to note that the decision of the Court of Criminal Appeal to quash Mr Nally's conviction for manslaughter had nothing to do with the 'social' issues at the heart of the unfortunate saga. The court made its decision on legal grounds and, in that sense, it was an eminently sensible verdict.

The purpose of a jury trial is that a defendant is allowed the opportunity to be found guilty or not guilty by his or her peers but Padraic Nally was denied that right. Instead, the jury was informed that the Mayo farmer's guilt was beyond doubt and they could only decide whether he should be convicted for murder or manslaughter. In the end, the jury opted for the lesser charge of manslaughter and Nally received a six-year prison sentence.

The grounds for appeal were as obvious as they were compelling and the decision of the Court of Criminal Appeal was entirely predictable. Of course, that did not make it any less surprising for the general public and, more particularly, for the family of John Ward.

Nonetheless, it is important to note that the decision had absolutely nothing to do with Irish attitudes to Travellers. Members of Traveller Support Groups were quick to express their dissatisfaction at the verdict and to imply that Mr Nally would not have walked free had he killed a member of the settled community. This is untrue. The acquittal of Mr Nally was based on legal grounds and it was the correct decision. The identity – or more importantly the ethnic grouping – of his victim was never a factor in the decision by the Court of Criminal Appeal and it was time for members of the various Traveller Support Groups to accept the ruling and stop turning the case into a socially-divisive football.

Immediately however, it was clear from the reaction of certain spokespersons for the Traveller community that, unfortunately, the battle-lines had been drawn for the retrial. One would have hoped the second trial would have been conducted in a less rancorous atmosphere that its predecessor.

The fact that Mr Ward was a member of the Traveller community should not have even been a matter for discussion. He was an intruder on Mr Nally's property – nothing more and nothing less. It was now up to a second jury to decide whether or not the Mayo farmer used excessive force in his dealings with Mr Ward.

A second trial was far from ideal but it was the only option open to the Court of Criminal Appeal. Undoubtedly, there were no winners in the first trial on either side. The second trial was unlikely to bring anything new to the table.

Chapter 13
Norfolk Farmer Tony Martin

The rain never stopped falling in August 1999 in Norfolk in the UK. For farmer Tony Martin, the conditions were less than ideal and it was difficult to get any work done outside. On the afternoon of August 19, when it became clear he wouldn't get any combine harvesting done for another day, Tony jumped in his car and went to visit his mother, who lived four miles away from his farmhouse near Wisbech.

Tony's mother was making salmon for dinner and she offered her son a plate. He looked at his watch and although the wafting aroma was tempting, he knew he needed to get home to Bleak House. Dusk was setting in and there were no lights in Bleak House at the time. The old powerline dated back to 1930 and had split outside. Tony had gotten into the habit of being home before it got too dark.

The 54-year-old bid his mother good night and began his journey back to Emneth Hungate. Pulling up outside his home, he left his keys in the ignition and went inside. It was dark by then and he had to feel his way up the stairs. Tony had managed to route an extension lead from one of the outside sheds up to his bedroom window on the first floor. Inside his bedroom, he switched on the lamp that he had linked to the external powerline and lay down on his bed.

Tony had been burgled a number of times prior to August 1999 – as recently as the previous May – and he had set about making it next to impossible for anyone to break into his house. Or so he thought.

"I had been doing bits and pieces of work on the house, changing around rooms and moving the staircase. I had also knocked some walls and doorways. I became very desperate when I was broken into the previous May so I got a drill and drilled big holes and put steel bars across the doors so that nobody could break in through the external doors. If you wanted to ram the door, you were going to have to ram the whole house down.

"I had one of those w-shaped ladders to get up the staircase. It sounds strange but it suited me and I was living there by myself. It was nobody else's business. I had made the house in such a way as you couldn't get in, unless you got a sledgehammer and knocked a hole in the wall," Mr Martin explained.

Lying on his bed that night, Tony was busily planning his chores for the following morning when he heard glass shattering downstairs.

Sixteen-year-old Fred Barras and 29-year-old Brendan Fearon were breaking into his house.

"They came in through a tiny kitchen window. It was double-glazed – not like the double-glaze you get nowadays; it was homemade double-glaze. Although I heard the noise, I had no idea what part of the house the noise was coming from, and at first, I lay there and tried to convince myself that maybe the house was falling down. The reality was someone was breaking into my house. I had been targeted by thieves again and I didn't know how many there were, what they intended to do, whether they were carrying weapons – I didn't know what to think," he recalled.

The shattering sound was followed by the noise of a zip opening. The intruders had brought a carrier bag with them and they were helping themselves to Tony's possessions downstairs.

"I was still lying on the bed; I didn't quite know what to do. Then I realised I couldn't just lie there. I was still fully clothed when they came into my house. Some people later tried to make out I was sitting waiting for them, but how was I to know I would be burgled that night? I almost always sleep with my clothes on. I have a habit when I'm busy of not taking off my clothes at night. When there's lots to be done on the farm, there's hardly any point, based on the few hours between when you get to sleep and when you get up the next morning. Because I was fully dressed, that led people to say I was prepared and waiting," he continued.

Tony realised he would have to get up and see what was going on in his house.

"I sat on the bed wondering what to do and realised I was going to have to go out through the bathroom, to the landing and try to understand what was happening downstairs."

At this point, he heard a tingle of aluminium.

"My little w-shaped ladder was made of aluminium. When I heard that noise, it really put the fear of life in me because that denoted to me that they were coming up the stairs. Whether they were or not, I don't know and I don't see it makes any difference. I scarpered back to the bedroom and stood at the other side of the bed where the window is. Then I got this beating sound in my ears – boom, boom, boom, boom. Whether it was adrenalin or my heart racing, I don't know. I couldn't stand it any longer. I didn't want anybody coming upstairs and cornering me. I decided I had to go downstairs."

Before he moved towards the landing, Tony grabbed his pump-action shotgun. He had never used it before – and didn't have a licence for the weapon – but in the heat of the moment, he made the decision that if he was going to confront intruders, he needed to be prepared.

"I defy anybody in my position, with what was happening to me, to do anything any different."

The following year, while serving a life sentence for the murder of Fred Barras, a fellow-prisoner made an interesting comment to the farmer. It's a statement that remains at the forefront of his mind, even all these years later – 'It is better to be judged by twelve than to be carried by six'.

Undoubtedly, Tony Martin feared for his life on that August night in 1999. He had no choice but to protect himself.

"It's very easy for people to say now that I shouldn't have went for my gun; that I shouldn't have fired it; but it's true what they say – you should never judge another man until you have been in his shoes," he reasoned.

That night, in a state of panic, Tony reached for his gun.

"I was a bit flummoxed and frantic because I couldn't find it at first but I managed to get a hold of it and went out of the room. I took a torch with me and headed for the staircase. I was going to shine the torch on the intruders to find out what was happening but they must've heard me on the staircase.

I had crept along as quietly as I could but it's an old house – dating back to the mid-1800s – with floorboards that creak. Nonetheless I crept along quietly. I didn't want them to know where I was; didn't want to blow my cover. At that stage, I didn't know if they had come up the stairs, if they were on the stairs, if they were hiding around a corner and were going to shoot me. I hadn't a clue what to expect," he explained.

Tony's torch didn't work.

"It was one of these PP9 torches and I've always found with all the PP9s I've ever bought, that when you go to switch them on first, they don't switch on. If you bang them against something, they come on, but I never got that far. Suddenly, the intruders were at the bottom of the stairs. They had a torch and shone it on me. I was blinded by the light. The rest is history. I pulled the trigger and nothing happened at first. The problem was, they could see me but I couldn't see them. I still didn't know if they had weapons. Then, I remembered it was a pump-action gun so when I moved it, it went bang and I just kept on firing the gun. I couldn't see what I was firing at," he added.

Believing he had scared away his intruders, Tony turned on his heels and went back upstairs.

"I figured nobody would want to approach me after that so I went back to my bedroom. I never heard anything else. I just sat on the bed and tried to make sense of it all but it was impossible."

Considering what had just happened in his home, it was no surprise that Tony found he could not relax and after a few minutes, he stood up again and went downstairs. His torch still wasn't working so he made his way through the passageways out to the car because he knew there was a torch in his car that was working. When he returned to his house and had a look in the breakfast room where the shots had been fired, there were no signs of anything unusual.

"Apparently there was blood but I didn't see any. The sash window was lying on the ground. It wasn't properly fitted at the time because I was making some changes around the house. They must have just pulled out the sash window and stepped over it to climb out. It wouldn't have been too difficult," he explained.

Tony then spotted a carrier bag on the ground. There were some of his possessions – pieces of silver – in the bag.

"I was nearly going to pick it up but then I told myself not to touch it. Although I didn't know what had happened at the time, if I had touched it, the prosecution could have said I put the silver in the bag to make it look as though they were stealing. I didn't touch anything. There were no obvious signs anybody had been shot," he said.

Taking his gun with him, Tony returned to his car and drove down the driveway, around the back of the orchard and back around to the front of his house.

"I had no inkling at that stage that I had shot anybody. What I also didn't know was that on the right-hand side in the shrubbery, there was a dead body. I had no idea I was going to have to deal with all of this over the next few days. I never intended to shoot anybody. I was on the staircase when I fired the gun and what killed Fred Barras was that he took the full shot. When you're not very far away from someone, they take the shot tight rather than wide," Tony explained.

The English farmer had been working on several projects around his house in the weeks and months leading up to the shooting. As a result of the construction work, there were bricks lying all around the floor downstairs.

"I didn't know if the intruders were going to pick up a brick and throw it at me or if they had a gun with them and were going to shoot me in my own house. I was on a survival course," he recalled.

Tony kept driving around for a while, trying to see if he could find the people who had broken into his house. He was sure they were hiding somewhere on his property. What he didn't realise was that Fearon had made his way to a neighbour's house, having been shot in the leg. His mate was lying dead on Martin's property.

The farmer proceeded to drive to his mother's house. She was fast asleep and he had to throw stones at the window to wake her. When Tony's mother emerged, he told her he had some trouble down the Hungate.

"I didn't like driving around with a gun so I left it in my mother's house. My mother made me a cup of coffee but I couldn't tell her what had happened, except that somebody had broken into the house and I had fired the gun. It was said later that I should have called the police but in 1999, mobile phones were fairly scarce. I had one of those fax machines with a telephone on it back at Bleak House but I hadn't called the police. I had picked up the phone and was going to dial 999 before I left the house but then I realised I had a problem. These guys had been in my house and they may have gone to the police and said someone had fired at them. I had used a gun without a licence, so basically it was a no-go. I put the phone down. I was that close to ringing the police but I didn't," he explained.

When Tony left his mother's house that night, he was afraid to go home. These hooligans had entered his house. They had frightened him, as he had been frightened so many times in the past. To an outsider, Tony's house was run-down and dilapidated. To Tony, his home was his castle.

Instead of returning to Bleak House that night, he checked into a local hotel. The following morning, the police had already been up to Emneth Hungate. When they didn't find him there, they moved the search down town and spotted his car. At that stage, they knew somebody had been shot but were unaware they still had to deal with a dead body.

Unfortunately, what had actually happened in those few moments on the night of August 19, 1999, was that Tony Martin had shot and injured Fred Barras and injured Brendan Fearon. The two men fled the scene in a flurry after the shots were fired but Fred Barras died as a result of the wounds. The severity of the situation only came to light a few days later.

On August 19, a wounded Fearon had made his way to a nearby house and alerted the police. He was taken to hospital and treated for his injuries. The following morning, the police arrested and interviewed Tony Martin.

"When I was first interviewed by the police, I still didn't know what had happened and nor did the police. They knew they had somebody in hospital who had been shot and they had interviewed him. Fearon told them he came to my door, knocked on it and I came out with my rottweilers – which is not true – and that he had told me he was looking for work. Fearon said that when I came out the front door with the dogs, he asked me to do something with them and that I said 'you needn't worry about the dogs' and then went bang, bang, bang and shot him. It's a blatant lie," he insisted.

From his hospital bed, Fearon did not initially tell the police that his friend had been shot. According to Tony Martin, Fearon didn't want to grass on Fred Barras and thought the 16-year-old had escaped.

That afternoon, Tony was charged with grievous bodily harm (GBH) on Brendan Fearon but as it turned out, there was more to follow.

"The police had been down on my farm investigating what had happened. My three dogs were roaming around and as the police were about to leave, one of my dogs stood beside the body of Fred Barras and then the whole situation completely changed."

On August 23, Tony Martin was still at the station when the police came into his cell and told him they were changing his charge. The body of Fred Barras had been found and Martin was now being charged with murder.

The following day, Mr Martin was remanded in custody at King's Inn Magistrates Court and on September 7, Judge David Mellor – at a 30-minute hearing behind closed doors at Norwich Crown Court – ruled that Tony Martin be freed on conditional bail.

Two days later, hundreds of mourners gathered for the funeral of Fred Barras in Nottinghamshire. Martin's bail was revoked and he was returned to Norwich Prison for his own protection.

On January 10, 2000, Fearon and Darren Bark – the driver that night – both from Newark, Nottinghamshire, admitted conspiring to burgle Bleak House, accompanied by Barras. Fearon was jailed for three years and Bark was sentenced to 30 months.

On April 10, Tony Martin denied murdering Barras and attempting to murder Fearon; wounding Fearon with intent to cause injury; and possessing a Winchester pump-action shotgun with intent to endanger life. Martin admitted not having a firearms licence.

Four days later, Norwich Crown Court heard that Tony Martin had been taken to a secure location, under police protection, after death threats were made against him. There were reports of a £60,000 price tag on his life.

On April 19, 2000, Tony Martin was jailed for life for the murder of Fred Barras, with 10 years to run concurrently for the wounding offence and a further 12 months for possession of an illegal firearm.

The following day his solicitor, Nick Makin, pledged to appeal against his client's conviction and Martin's legal team claimed a female juror had reportedly called an independent Norfolk radio station claiming she and others had received threats during the trial.

On April 21, the independent Broadlands 102FM radio station in Norwich insisted the woman who contacted the station did not mention being threatened. Tony Jones, an uncle of Fred Barras, denied anybody connected to the teenager's family made any attempt to intimidate jurors.

On April 26, the family of one of the jurors told the BBC that members of the jury believed they were being stared at by people in the public gallery and felt afraid leaving the court. Martin's legal team pledged to pursue the claims to the Court of Appeal in an attempt to get their client's murder conviction quashed.

On July 27, Mr Justice Curtis granted permission for Martin to appeal against his conviction. After replacing his legal team, Mr Martin launched a new appeal against his murder conviction in August 2001, claiming he was not properly represented at his trial. Meanwhile, his supporters appealed for funds to help fight his murder conviction.

On October 15, 2001, Michael Wolkind, Queen's Counsel (QC), who was heading up Mr Martin's new legal team, told the Court of Appeal that his trial lawyers had not presented Mr Martin's own account of what happened. Mr Wolkind argued that there was 'compelling' evidence to show the farmer acted in self-defence and under provocation or diminished responsibility.

On October 30 that year, Tony Martin's murder conviction was reduced to manslaughter, and his 10-year sentence for wounding Fearon was cut to three years, to run concurrently.

Despite bids for early release in January 2003, Tony Martin was eventually released from prison on July 28 that year. Mr Martin was delighted to have his freedom back but remains adamant that he should never have been jailed.

"When you pick up a gun, you've got to be prepared to use it. Some people would say that's incriminating but if you're confronted by the unknown, the best thing you can have is a gun. I said, before my trial, there would be no winners. I would like to be better known for something else, rather than to be known for shooting people. The reality though is that I was targeted by career criminals. People were sick and tired of theft at the time. People were – and still are – being randomly targeted in their homes and it seems to me we've got this duty of care to bloody criminals in this country," added Mr Martin.

Tony Martin was in his own home, minding his business, when thieves targeted his property. When he shot and killed one of the intruders, he became the criminal in the eyes of the law.

His case prompted national debate on the measures homeowners could take to protect themselves. Martin's actions were vilified by some but more widely vindicated, with many – including Charlton Heston, the actor and president of the US National Rifle Association – supporting his right to protect his property.

Locally, the Free Tony Martin campaign gathered followers quickly.

"It was an automatic reaction. It touched a nerve with ordinary decent people. MPs and newspapers received up to 1,000 letters from people – the majority in my favour – saying it was an outrage I had been trialled for murder and then convicted."

Tony received thousands of letters in prison.

"I have a cottage with about 15 of Her Majesty's polythene bags full of letters I received when I was in jail. The letters and the messages gave me strength and fortitude. When I was locked up, there would be up to 70 letters a day. At Christmas 2000, I received 4,000 Christmas cards. I don't know if the Queen gets that many," he added.

Prior to August 1999, Tony Martin had a number of break-ins at Bleak House. He had chased an intruder once when he was in his late 30s. The criminal had released the loot along the way.

"I had a number of break-ins before then but there was nothing serious. On one occasion, the thief got hold of a pillowcase and used it as swag-bag, taking watches and other bits which I considered my grandmother's heirlooms. They were of sentimental value," he noted.

After being targeted on so many occasions, Tony was at his wits' end.

"I had said to somebody 'if I catch anybody in my home again, I'll shoot them' – that was used against me but it was something that I said in desperation. It's a metaphor, I didn't mean it. I never set out to shoot or kill anybody. You hear people saying about their children 'I'll murder him if he does this or that' – they don't mean it. It was unfair to use that against me," he said.

Now, all these years later, Tony still has no faith in the legal system in the UK. After the incident, Mr Martin wrote to David Cameron telling him he wanted a public enquiry on the matter.

"I'm a very misunderstood man and my mouth has incriminated me in lots of ways. I want a public enquiry, there are many questions to be answered. People have been let down in this country. It should be like in America, you should be safe in your house. You should have a basic right to feel safe and protected in your own home. If criminals know you have the right to pick up a gun to protect yourself, they might go and do something else instead of targeting innocent victims," he said.

"If my case happened in America, you wouldn't be allowed to be judged because they wouldn't bring the charge. Representatives of the National Rifle Association of America have been to see me several times. They came to see me in prison too; they couldn't understand what was going on here," he added.

While Tony Martin felt somewhat vindicated to have his murder conviction reduced to manslaughter, he still maintains he shouldn't have been convicted in the first place.

"It's not a matter of people 'getting off', it's about being 'acquitted' – not being guilty in the first place. People from Scotland told me if it had happened there, I'd never have been charged with murder, it would have been manslaughter. Fearon was also trying to sue me at one stage but you can't do that anymore. If somebody injures themselves in your home – if you, as the burglar are injured by the homeowner – you can't sue anymore because you're committing a crime," he pointed out.

After the shooting at his home in August 1999, Tony Martin never set foot inside Bleak House again. He still visits his property to attend to duties outside but the home he once loved has been tarnished by the events on August 19 that year.

"After coming out of prison, I never stepped inside my house again. It was my home but the whole world had been in my home during the investigation. In the courtroom, there were pictures of my staircase and pictures of various rooms inside my house. I must admit, it did look a bit of a mess in the photographs but the bottom line is, this was my house, it was nobody else's business. Are we trying a man for the way he lives or are we trying a man in relation to the situation he found himself in?" he questioned.

"I go to the farm every day but I don't enter the house. It's a shame really but it was inevitable what was going to happen. The police are doing nothing and they can't. The numbers in the Force have been decimated."

In May 2013, Tony Martin was faced with another burglar at his property in Emneth Hungate. The farmer was checking his outbuildings when he came across the intruder. He claimed the man, in his 20s, had a £90 tractor battery and a new sink unit in his arms.

The would-be burglar drove away when confronted, but Mr Martin told police he decided not to attempt to detain the intruder.

"There were items in the shed that could have been used as weapons so, if I had wanted to fight him off, I could have. I wished I had but after everything I had been through in the past I just couldn't face all that hassle again. It wasn't the first time it had happened since I got out of prison – it has happened two or three times – but I couldn't do anything, I didn't want to be made out as a criminal again," he said.

At the Conservative Party conference in October 2002, the Justice Secretary Chris Grayling said householders who react with force would be given more legal protection. Mr Grayling said 'grossly disproportionate' force would continue to be illegal but added that the bar would be higher than the current 'proportionate' force test used in courts.

In April 2013, a law finally came into being in the UK to give householders the right to 'bash a burglar', but with a string of exemptions attached. For example, people will not be protected if they chase the burglar outside – and any fight must take place indoors.

Of course, in Tony Martin's case, the confrontation did take place indoors but nonetheless, his actions were criminalised by the legal system in the UK at the time. To this day, Mr Martin believes he acted in the only way he could on that fateful night. He was confronted by career criminals in his own home and he had to defend himself and his property. Mr Martin didn't know what he was dealing with when intruders entered his home, near Wisbech, and he had no idea whether he would live to see the morning of August 20, 1999.

"I felt I had no option but to protect myself. I never intended to shoot or kill anybody. I thought the shots would just frighten them away. I can't take back what happened that night and I'm sorry that the Barras family lost their son. But at the end of the day, it goes back to that statement made to me while I was in prison: It is better to be judged by twelve than to be carried by six."

Chapter 14
Nally's Retrial in Dublin

When Padraic Nally's manslaughter conviction was sensationally quashed in October 2006, there was much speculation about a date for the retrial. It was generally accepted that the following April would the likely choice but less than two months after the acquittal, the same faces gathered in Dublin.

On Monday, December 4, 2006, a jury of eight men and four women were sworn in for the retrial of Padraic Nally at Dublin's Four Courts. The defendant was dressed in a navy pinstripe suit, with a blue shirt and a navy tie. The jury was warned that they must deal with the case strictly on the evidence given in the trial.

The evidence in the retrial was largely the same as that which had been heard in the courthouse in Castlebar in July 2005 but at the retrial, Padraic Nally was not called to give evidence. There were mixed views among the reporters present. Some believed the defendant needed to stand before the jury to tell his story. Others felt Padraic Nally's evidence at the initial trial in Castlebar was, ironically, far too honest.

For anybody who had ever been present in a courtroom before, it was clear the evidence given by the accused at the initial trial in Castlebar was incredibly honest; perhaps to a fault. Mr Nally's telling of the incident and his striking of John 'Frog' Ward was not like anything that had been heard in a courtroom before.

The farmer had told the initial trial he had struck the deceased repeatedly with a stick – "It was like hitting a stone or a badger. You could hit him but you could not kill him."

But regardless of whether or not Padraic Nally took the stand at the retrial in Dublin and regardless of whether the jury were from Mayo – as in his initial trial – or from the Capital, there wasn't a person in the country who was not already familiar with the evidence given at the trial in Castlebar in July 2005. There was no need to go over old ground once again.

Twenty-year-old Tom Ward gave evidence on the stand in Dublin and said he had been with his father at Padraic Nally's farmyard at Funshinaugh, Cross, on October 14, 2004. Mr Nally, according to Tom, had 'fucked up' the lives of the Ward family.

Addressing the court, Tom explained that since his father's death, he had suffered from memory loss and had tried to take his own life on a number of occasions.

"I slit my wrists, took an overdose and tried to drive into a river. I got bangs on the head in the crash. Since then, I find it hard to remember some things," he told the jury.

Tom said he had spent a good deal of time with his father, as together they operated a business buying and selling cars. Under questioning by Paul O'Higgins, Senior Counsel for the prosecution, Tom told the court that on the morning of October 14, 2004, he had driven his father to the hospital in Galway, where he had a day-care appointment at the Psychiatric Department.

"He wasn't well and he was on a lot of medication," Tom pointed out.

However, under cross-examination by Mr Brendan Grehan, Senior Counsel for the defence, Ward said he had no idea that his father had been hearing voices, telling him to kill himself and his wife. He also denied that his father was a violent man and said he had no knowledge of his father being involved in bare-knuckle fighting.

Mr Grehan listed some of John Ward's 80 previous convictions to his son, including threatening Gardaí with a slash-hook, but Tom claimed he was not aware of the majority of the offences. It later emerged that Tom had been with his father on the occasion when the slash-hook was produced.

On the day of the killing, Tom and John had decided to 'take a spin and drive around' to see if they could find any vehicles for sale. With

Tom driving, the pair drove towards the village of Cross and John told his son to take a left turn off the main road, which led to Funshinaugh.

Tom, who had a criminal record and was serving an 11-month sentence for possession of an offensive weapon at the time of the retrial, told the court that his father spotted a car outside a house on October 14, 2004, that they now know to be Padraic Nally's residence. Tom told the court he reversed into the driveway and his father got out to knock at the door to see if the owner was home. Hearing a noise outside, Mr Nally came out of the house and approached the car.

"He walked up to me and said 'who's gone in there?' I told him that it was my father and that he was looking for the owner. Mr Nally turned around and said: 'he won't be coming out alive'," Mr Ward told the court.

Later, under cross-examination by Mr Grehan, Mr Ward was forced to admit the word 'alive' was not used by Mr Nally and had not been brought into evidence prior to this.

Mr Ward appeared confused when he was asked about his business of buying and selling cars with his father and was not able to say how long he had been in business or how many cars he had bought. He admitted that when he bought cars, he didn't tend to have them registered and as a result, they could not be traced back to him.

The court heard that on the day in question, neither Tom nor his father had any money with them, even though they were allegedly looking to buy a car.

Tom said he had never been in the Funshinaugh area prior to October 14, 2004. He told the court he and his father had stopped at John Murphy's house before coming to Nally's and said he had no knowledge of what his father and Mr Murphy spoke about. However, the court heard that Mr Murphy had been suspicious of the two Travellers and took note of their vehicle registration number.

Leaving the stand, Tom made a final appeal to the Court.

"We've lost our father, all we're asking for is a fair trial," he said.

***

Following the shooting on the afternoon of October 14, Mr Nally drove to his neighbour's house to tell him what had just occurred. Mr

Nally didn't have a telephone at his home and wanted to call the Gardaí from Michael Varley's house. In the Central Criminal Court in Dublin, the jury heard that Mr Nally had appeared nervous, agitated and short of breath when he called Claremorris Garda Station and spoke to Garda Pauline Golden at 2.20pm.

Mr Nally said two men had come into his property to 'rob' him. One got into a van and drove off and he had shot 'the other fellow'.

"He said 'I think he's dead, he isn't moving'," Garda Golden told the court.

Continuing, she explained that she then alerted Sergeant Carroll in Ballinrobe, as well as Sergeant Murray and Inspector Fitzmaurice, before calling the ambulance, Dr Regan and Fr Kilcoyne.

Prior to the incident, Mr Varley was at home and noticed a car on the road. He recognised the driver as John Ward, whom he had seen on the road near his home the previous day. A short time later, Mr Nally had come to Varley's house and told him he was 'in bother'. After making a number of calls, the neighbours returned to Mr Nally's house and soon after, the emergency services arrived.

Mr Varley said his neighbour was pale and had blood on his hands. He appeared calm but shocked. Mr Nally briefly told him what had happened and Mr Varley didn't ask any questions.

Under cross-examination by Mr Michael Bowman, Barrister for the defence, Mr Varley said the area was rural and that most farmers held down jobs. There would not be many people about during the day. He spoke highly of Padraic Nally and said that if he ever needed anything, Nally would drop all tools and come to help.

Mr Varley said his neighbour had been 'demented with fear' since his chainsaw was stolen the previous February and noted that he was always on edge because there was a history of old people being assaulted in their homes in rural Ireland. He told the court that Padraic was not a violent man and was popular at marts in Claremorris, Ballinrobe, Maam Cross and Athenry.

State Pathologist Professor Marie Cassidy gave similar evidence to that given at the initial trial in Castlebar. She told the jury at the Central Criminal Court in Dublin that it was the gunshot wound to

John Ward's heart that proved fatal. Professor Cassidy carried out the examination at the scene of the incident in Funshinaugh on October 14, 2004.

She said Mr Ward had two gunshot wounds, one in the right loin area and another, which began in the left armpit and entered the right side of the victim's chest inside his upper left arm. The bullet from the single-barrel shotgun – which was shown to the court – tracked through the upper arm and into his chest, through his rib cage, puncturing his lung and damaging the pericardial sac surrounding the heart. It was the loss of blood from this gunshot wound that killed Mr Ward.

The court heard that in addition to the gunshots, Mr Ward had received 10 blows to the head, which had been inflicted with a long, fairly narrow instrument; likely to be made of wood.

Professor Cassidy gave a detailed description of the various lacerations that were discovered on Mr Ward's body and noted that the initial bullet wound would have been painful but would not necessarily have caused the victim to collapse.

She told the court that Mr Ward had suffered a fractured arm and suggested that this would probably have been caused as a result of Mr Ward raising him arms to defend himself.

Professor Cassidy said the gunman would have fired the fatal shot while standing at a higher level than the victim but she admitted that the shot may have been fired while Mr Ward was bending over or crouching on the roadway.

The jury was shown three pictures of Mr Ward's body, as it was found at the scene on October 14.

Unlike the original trial, Padraic Nally chose not to take the stand during the retrial at the Central Criminal Court, sitting in Dublin's Four Courts. Instead, Sergeant James Carroll relayed the statements made by Mr Nally. Under cross-examination by Brendan Grehan, Sergeant Carroll admitted that Mr Nally had been very forthcoming when he spoke to the Gardaí and was always pleasant in his dealings with the Gardaí.

In his statements and interviews, Mr Nally had described spending time in his hayshed watching out for intruders. He had not been sleeping well at night and cried when his sister returned to her North Mayo residence the previous Sunday night. Mr Nally had spoken of a great sense of fear and panic during interviews and he was described in court as 'honest and upright'.

The court also heard of the locality's crime statistics and of two particular incidents in Mayo where elderly people had been killed in their homes – the case of the Gilmore brothers in Thomastown, outside Kilmaine, and the case of Eddie Fitzmaurice in Charlestown.

In questioning Sergeant Carroll, Mr Grehan took the court through a list of John Ward's 80 previous convictions and offences, including a list of burglary and larceny offences, as well as trespassing, handling stolen goods, assault on Gardaí and malicious damage.

The jury also heard that, prior to his death, the deceased was awaiting trial on two separate incidents after he threatened Gardaí with a slash-hook. There were also four warrants outstanding for the arrest of Mr Ward.

Garda Pauric Deery from the Divisional Scenes of Crime Unit in Castlebar told the court that he and two colleagues had been called to Sandyhill Halting Site in Charlestown in April 2002, investigating Mr Ward's involvement in the theft of a fireplace. On this occasion, Mr Ward had waved a slash-hook at the Gardaí and the three officers were forced to leave the scene and return later with armed members.

Summing up the prosecution case, Mr Paul O'Higgins argued that Mr Nally intended death and not serious injury.

"Mr Nally intended that John Ward should die," he told the jury.

Continuing, he stated that Padraic Nally could only be innocent if the jury was to believe he killed John Ward in self-defence and if the members believed Mr Nally judged the situation objectively and used no more force than was reasonably necessary to protect his own life.

The argument of self-defence, according to Mr O'Higgins, simply did not stand up to scrutiny. He urged the jury to set aside whatever sympathy they might feel for Padraic Nally at the time of the shooting and judge the case based on the facts presented.

"Mr Nally said he was in a state of terror and fear but there are certain things about the killing that suggest he wasn't terribly frightened or worried. He was worrying about whether he'd get the gun back."

Addressing the jury, Mr O'Higgins pointed out that perhaps a killing in provocation is enough to reduce a murder charge to one of manslaughter but stressed that provocation is not enough reason to find Mr Nally innocent.

"Maybe he only slept an hour the night before and his nerves were in a frizzle but that provocation could only reduce murder to manslaughter," he stated.

"Whatever you think of John Ward and his record, that record was unknown to Mr Nally at the time, even if he thought he looked like a 'rough customer'. This is not a killing which happened by accident or occurred in self-defence and even if you think there was some self-defence involved, this cannot be seen as an innocent killing and must amount to manslaughter," argued Mr O'Higgins.

Mr Brendan Grehan said he was a little surprised to see his 'learned friend' refer to murder, pointing out that a murder charge was not on the table.

"You're not fools, you live in the real world but nonetheless, it won't help you to refer back to the previous trial. The prosecution had a nerve to refer to that. There's another matter too, where the prosecution referred to the fact that this wasn't an 'innocent killing'. This was an attempt by the prosecution to cause some confusion, where an accused person is presumed innocent. No jury ever has the power to determine if someone is innocent. The jury's job is to determine if the prosecution has proven the defendant is guilty. Mr O'Higgins quoted selectively and extensively from statements. I don't propose to do the same; it would be an idle exercise," said Mr Grehan.

Continuing, the Senior Counsel for the defence noted the reoccurring theme throughout the statements that his client was acting in fear, panic and terror when he killed Mr Ward.

"What are the circumstances whereby a 60-year-old law-abiding man comes to shoot another man dead?" he asked.

"Whatever insecurities had developed in his mind on that fateful day, Mr Nally did not stir outside his doors to look for trouble; trouble came to him. A greater contrast between two individuals couldn't be found and that's relevant in your assessment of the facts and what the Wards were doing at Mr Nally's house that day.

You can buy Tom Ward's story that they were out on a random spin looking for cars after Tom Ward's hospital appointment but it's a story and an account that doesn't hold water," he reasoned.

Addressing the jury, Mr Grehan said his client had been targeted by thieves in the past. "They stole much more than physical possessions; they stole his peace of mind. Mr Nally was getting more and more concerned about his safety and had moved his antique weapon out of his house to his hayshed, 60 yards away, because he feared someone would come into his house in the middle of the night and use it on him."

Arguing that Mr Nally should be found not guilty of manslaughter, Mr Grehan said the incidents of October 14, 2004, occurred in a matter of minutes and said the basic human instinct is to survive.

"When you're in really great fear, where you think you might not survive, you cannot act rationally. Mr Nally was 'out of his mind with fear'. He was acting in self-defence and if you act reasonably in self-defence, you are entitled to acquittal. A homeowner has to make split-second judgements. It's all very well in the cold light of day to say Mr Nally could have went to the Gardaí. He reacted in a basic manner out of fear. The defence says Mr Nally was acting in self-defence."

***

For Padraic Nally, an honest and decent South Mayo farmer, the two years leading up to the retrial had been nothing short of traumatic and it had been a long fortnight for all involved.

62-year-old Padraic Nally began his ordeal in Dublin on Sunday, December 3, when he, his supporters and his legal team arrived in the capital for the manslaughter trial. A typical countryman, used to spending his mornings, afternoons and evenings walking his 65-acre farm in Funshinaugh, Cross, it was no surprise that Padraic Nally felt out of place on Dublin's busy streets. But, his anxiety and wariness at his pending trial was somewhat lessened by the overwhelming messages of support that flowed in from well-wishers from all across the country.

Padraic had never spent much time in Dublin and following the second day of his trial at the Four Courts, his solicitor and confidante Sean Foy took the Nally siblings on a walk through the city. For Padraic, this voyage was an adventure in itself and having never set foot on

Grafton Street prior to this, Padraic was astounded to find that every second person was eager to shake his hand, pat him on the back and wish him the very best in his trial.

Men and women of all ages and from every walk of life gathered around the retiring Mayo man and in messages from the heart, extended their very best wishes to him.

On the roadways, cars and vans honked their horns and waved their support to the shell-shocked farmer. Padraic could hardly believe that so many people were so keen to boost his morale and he was moved by the sincerity of the people of Ireland. But there was more to come.

Back in O'Shea's Merchant, where Padraic and his supporters were staying for the duration of the retrial, the diners at lunch and dinnertime made real efforts to stop briefly at Padraic's table, with further messages of encouragement. One lady was so sympathetic to the plight of the farmer that she insisted on picking up the tab for Padraic and his fellow-diners as they sat for their meal one evening.

Since that fateful afternoon on Mr Nally's farm on October 14, 2004, life had dramatically changed for Padraic and during his initial trial and his 11 months in prison, Padraic's friends and neighbours never let him down. From their presence in the Castlebar Courthouse to their visits to the prison, the loyal group were by his side whenever possible. In addition, with the help of Padraic's sister, the Padraic Nally Support Group took on the huge task of maintaining the Nally farm and looking after his home and yard, outside the village of Cross in South Mayo.

In Dublin during Mr Nally's seven-day trial, these supporters were back in force and because of their love and respect for the 62-year-old farmer, they had put their own lives on hold, prepared to stay with him for as long as he needed their help.

Up to 30 of Padraic's friends and neighbours could be found in Court No. 2 at the Four Courts on any of the seven trying days during the retrial, and with almost as large a group of journalists present, together with the Gardaí, witnesses, opposing legal teams and many interested parties from within the legal fraternity, the courtroom was bulging on many occasions.

From beginning to end, Padraic's only sister was at his side and although her heart was almost breaking, Maureen was adamant she would put on a brave face and help her brother through his trial. The quiet and unassuming pair provided one another with practical and emotional support during the two long weeks in Dublin and were there for each other through the highs and lows.

On the afternoon when the jury retired to consider the verdict, there was a general feeling that it may take the eight men and four women until morning to reach a decision, but as the hours slipped by and days turned to nights, it became increasingly clear this jury was not rushing into a rash decision.

Charging the Dublin jury, Judge Kevin O'Higgins advised them that they were required to approach the case in a 'cold, clinical, dispassionate, objective, calm fashion' and assured them that they should not feel that they were under any time constraints.

"It would be quite wrong to say 'there's the decent Mr Nally and isn't the country plagued with Travellers'. Your business is to decide the case according to the evidence and the law. Your business is to bring in a true verdict. You should not decide the case on your sympathy with Mr Nally or your views on Travellers," warned Judge O'Higgins, before he sent them to consider the evidence at 3.25pm on Tuesday, December 12.

After one hour and 23 minutes, the frustrated 12 called for a cigarette break and returned a little refreshed. At 7.15pm, the jury members were sent to their hotel after three hours and 28 minutes of deliberations. Court resumed at 10.30am on Wednesday, with Judge O'Higgins telling the dozen Dubliners that if they could not reach a unanimous verdict, they would be allowed to return a majority verdict of 10-2 or 11-1.

Before heading back to their room, the foreman asked the judge if he would assist them in reading through the evidence of Michael Varley and also that of Tom Ward. Judge O'Higgins duly obliged.

By lunchtime, the jury had been deliberating for five hours and seven minutes and retired for their well-deserved meal. A short break in the afternoon was all the time that the jury had to relax and by Wednesday evening, they were once again off to their hotel, following nine hours and 56 minutes of contemplation.

Although nobody knew what the day held in store, Thursday was to be the last morning that the large Mayo crowd would descend on the Four Courts and after lunch and 12 hours and one minute of deliberations, Judge O'Higgins advised the jury that it was possible for them to return a non-verdict. However, the eight men and four women were not giving up that easily and while most people figured that the case would close with a Hung Jury, the 12 were by no means finished.

Returning to Court at 4.12pm, the foreman of the jury posed a question relating to the location of the Biggins' household and even after an hour of searching through the transcripts, the judge was unable to offer a definitive answer, based on the evidence heard during the trial. Nevertheless, it was becoming increasingly clear that the jury was in for the long haul and there was a feeling among Mr Nally's supporters that this question was suggesting the jury members were leaning towards an acquittal. However, nobody could be sure what was really going on behind closed doors and many wished they could be a fly-on-the-wall in the jury room, even just for a few moments.

The large supporting contingent from Mayo were on edge as they awaited the decision, the battling legal teams were beginning to feel the pressure and the jury was desperately working towards the hugely-anticipated outcome. But, although the entire crowd was restless and nervous as they listened closely for the final knock from the jury room, nobody was as apprehensive or concerned as Padraic Nally.

For the Mayo farmer, and indeed for his sister Maureen, it had been a long and tiring fortnight. The stress of the potentially life-changing court case had taken its toll on the popular farmer, landing him in hospital with chest pains for almost 24 hours in the middle of the trial.

As evening drew near, family and friends on either side of the case began to wonder if the jury would continue its deliberations into Friday and perhaps even beyond the weekend. But they needn't have worried. They didn't have long to wait.

Shortly after 6.10pm on Thursday evening, a faint knock from the jury room sent waves of anxiety across the courtroom. Many who had taken a short stroll were quickly alerted to the latest development. All eyes were on the registrar. Had the jury simply requested a cigarette break? Had they given up their argument and opted for a non-verdict? Or, had the time really come for Nally's fate to be sealed for once and for all?

In the minutes that followed, as the crowd made their way back to the courtroom, eyes darted across the room, as journalists and supporters attempted to lip-read from the mouths of the registrar and opposing legal teams. Soon, the message was clear. A verdict had been returned and in a matter of moments, Padraic Nally would be faced with one of two very different paths.

Padraic and Maureen returned to their seats, spots which had become familiar to them over the previous two weeks. The siblings kept their heads down, anxious and afraid about what they were going to hear. At 6.15pm, following 15 hours and 32 minutes of deliberations, the judge returned to court and called for the jury. The relief on the faces of the 12 was plain to see, but they still weren't giving anything away. The jury members were simply delighted to have reached a conclusion on their mammoth task and at last, they would be going home to their own families and loved ones.

An eerie silence fell over the courtroom. Nobody knew what to think or how to feel. "Have at least 10 of you reached a verdict on count number one?" asked the registrar.

The foreman paused. Hearts raced.

"Not guilty" he said at last.

It took a moment for the news to sink in and as the judge excused the jury, thanking them for their care and consideration, Padraic Nally continued to focus on a spot on the ground. Maureen and Padraic sat in a solemn silence and it was only when Brendan Grehan approached his client, put his hand on Padraic's shoulder and uttered "It's over now," that the Mayo farmer believed what he had heard.

Padraic's legal team gathered around and as Paddy Rock and Michael Varley made their way towards him, the 62-year-old could no longer fight the tears. Beside him, Maureen too let her emotions out and as Padraic's closest friends embraced him with tears in their eyes, the courtroom erupted into a mobile-frenzy, with text messages flying across the lines and various ringtones alerting the crowd to their phone calls. There was only one thing on everybody's mind and as the answer button was hit on the many phones, two words echoed across the room …"Not Guilty".

Chapter 15
Kilbeggan Pensioner Christy Hanley

The killing of Kilbeggan pensioner Christy Hanley in 2008 shook the Co Westmeath village to its very core. The 83-year-old was robbed, beaten and left for dead at his small cottage on Bridge Street in Kilbeggan on May 21, 2008. An estimated €10,000 in cash was stolen from Mr Hanley's home and 47-year-old Noel Cawley of no fixed abode, but with a previous address in Castleblayney, Co Monaghan, was later convicted.

A jury at the Central Criminal Court found Cawley guilty of manslaughter and robbery. He was sentenced to 16 years in prison.

Throughout the investigation, and again during the nine-day trial, Cawley was uncooperative. He denied the murder and robbery of Mr Hanley, pleading not guilty to all charges. According to Cawley, he had nothing whatsoever to do with Mr Hanley's demise and had no involvement in any associated crime.

The court heard that Cawley bound Mr Hanley's feet and hands, before beating him around his head and body. Before he left the house, with the cash he had stolen from the victim, Cawley put a coat over Mr Hanley's head. The victim was not dead when Cawley walked out the door but he died a number of hours later, frightened and alone, after choking on his own blood.

Mr Justice Patrick McCarthy, presiding over the trial, reduced the murder charge to manslaughter, taking the view that there was 'a reasonable possibility' Cawley did not intend to cause serious harm.

Nonetheless, he stated that even if the robbery had not resulted in Mr Hanley's death, it was of the utmost seriousness, pointing out that Mr Hanley suffered multiple blows to his head, shoulders, arms and legs, with his hands and feet tied.

Mr Justice McCarthy said Mr Hanley – a well-known horse dealer – had received a large amount of money in the days before his death and Cawley was seen with an estimated €10,000 in cash just hours after the killing. Mr Hanley was known to keep cash in his house but only one €5 note was found at the scene when his body was discovered the next morning.

The court heard that there was one modest mitigating factor for Cawley. He had telephoned the Gardaí at 9am the following morning to tell them Mr Hanley was tied up in his house. Of course, Cawley did not identify himself on the phone but he was seen making the call. This was the one and only time during the investigation that Cawley was of any assistance to the Gardaí.

The death of Mr Hanley in May 2008 shocked the entire community. Christy was a character in Kilbeggan. A settled itinerant, he was a popular trader and well-known horse dealer. He had something of an innocent charm and sadly, he knew his killer.

According to local retired Garda Jim O'Keefe, Cawley had been staying in the area for a couple of weeks prior to the incident.

"Cawley was kind of a Knight of the Road and was staying locally at the time with a guy called Paddy Rattigan. Paddy was known as the 'Soldier Rattigan', although he had never been in the army and I don't know how he got the name. The Soldier was harmless, not a criminal by any means but he knew Cawley and had given him a place to stay for a few weeks," recalled Mr O'Keefe.

Jim O'Keefe was the local Garda in Kilbeggan from 1991 until January 2008; a few short months before Mr Hanley's death. When he was first stationed in Kilbeggan, he and his family built a house less than a mile outside the town and so, although he had transferred to the traffic corps that January, he was still regarded by many as the local Garda.

The first breakthrough in the case came when a local taxi man telephoned Jim O'Keefe at home the night after the killing to tell him he had seen Christy and Cawley in a pub called The Black Kettle the previous night. Following this report, many others came forward with similar sightings and Cawley became the main suspect in the case.

"They were seen on a number of occasions drinking together on May 21. Christy had received a sizeable sum of cash around 10 days before his death. The talk was that he had sold a horse for €10,000 but regardless of whether he did or not, Christy would have had a steady stream of cash coming in all the time and he always kept a lot of money at his house. Cawley knew he had money."

It was Mr Hanley's decency, generosity and innocence that ultimately led to his death.

"Christy was very sociable; he'd sit down and talk to anyone and buy a drink for anyone who wanted one. With a few drinks on him, he'd take out a wad of cash – not in a boastful way, he just never had a wallet and wouldn't expect that anyone would be taking any notice of how much money he was carrying. That was his downfall. Cawley would have seen the cash that night and possibly Christy would have told him about the horse he had sold. It would have been innocence on Christy's part but he wouldn't have suspected that Cawley was taking notes," the retired Garda explained.

There was no forced entry into Mr Hanley's house that night and Gardaí believe Cawley returned to the house with his victim, possibly on the promise of another drink.

"The investigating Gardaí believed the two men went back to Christy's house together. The robbery was pre-meditated but whether or not the killing was pre-meditated is hard to know. The autopsy showed Christy was alive for a few hours after Cawley left. Cawley made a call to the Gardaí the following morning and as far as I recall, he was caught on CCTV making that phone call," Mr O'Keefe continued.

Family and friends of Mr Hanley were relieved to see the perpetrator brought to justice but said sadly, it wouldn't bring Christy back.

Mr Hanley had been living alone in his home since the death of his sister, Hannah, two years earlier. Hannah's death had shook Christy.

"They were very close all their lives and lived in the family home, just up the road from the distillery on Bridge Street. There was an acre garden behind the house, with a hay shed and an orchard at the end of the garden. Christy dealt in horses. He kept some horses there and also had bits of land that he'd buy – two or three acres here and there, all scattered around the place – and he'd keep horses on these plots too," explained Mr O'Keefe.

"Christy and Hannah were settled itinerants; they were well settled. Their late mother was a trader. She had a pony and trap and went house-to-house selling blankets, pillow cases, rosary beads and crucifixes. That's the life Christy and Hannah knew. They weren't beggars, they were traders; hard-working people."

As well as dealing in horses and placing the odd bet, Christy and Hannah were regular race-goers.

"They'd go along to all the races and set up a roulette table; trick-of-the-loop stuff. Hannah would go around selling balloons and plastic toys; that was another part of their business. Christy always wore the trilby hat, with a little jacket and waistcoat but on days that he went to the races, he'd wear his red silk waistcoat and a white shirt and dickie bow. I think he thought he was adding a Las Vegas feel to the day."

The retired Garda recalled his own arrival in Kilbeggan in 1991 at a time when there had been a spate of burglaries among the elderly in the area.

"There was a lot of encouragement to get elderly people to put their money in a Bank or Post Office or Credit Union at the time, so I went to see Christy and he told me there was no way he'd put his money into an account. A few days later, I was talking to a publican in Kilbeggan and he told me that, as far as he knew, Christy had his money in the Credit Union some years before that but the Revenue discovered it and he got hit for tax so that was the end of it, he thought it was safer to have it at home. He was old-fashioned like that."

Christy's money wasn't under the mattress though, it was hidden in biscuit tins all around the house; in the sheds; and even under the apple trees in the orchard.

"The story used to go that local kids would come across one of these tins and they'd take a fiver or a tenner and then put the biscuit tin back. Christy was like a little savings bank for them or somewhere to go for a bit of pocket money if they could find one of the biscuit tins," Mr O'Keefe recalled.

The violent attack on Mr Hanley in May 2008 wasn't the first time the pensioner was targeted in a random attack for gain.

"He was robbed at least once before. He was assaulted on his way home, it was after a big race meet in Leopardstown or the Curragh. Christy had stopped off at The Volunteer Inn for a drink on the way home and, like the night in May 2008, he took a wad of money from his pocket to buy a drink. We believe he was targeted because of this. That was in the late 90s. He was roughed up and robbed as he walked home from the pub that night and he was really upset about the whole affair. We never found out how much money was taken because he was very reluctant to tell us anything. It was only that Hannah told us that we got wind of it at all. After that, he was very suspicious and superstitious. He decided the house was cursed so he lived out in the hay shed for a while."

Mr Hanley's reluctance to tell the Gardaí about the incident was by no means a slight on members of the Force. He had the utmost respect for the Gardaí and, according to Mr O'Keefe, you always got a welcome at Christy's door … even if you were arriving to serve a summons having caught him driving without tax or insurance.

"He always addressed me as sir, never as Garda," Mr O'Keefe noted.

"He had a lovely way about him, an innocent charm – albeit an innocent guilty charm sometimes – but he was a likeable rogue. He bred and trained horses and knew his trade inside out. Christy never married, nor did Hannah. They never regarded themselves as Travellers, they were business people, old-fashioned itinerants. He was as honest as the day was long in many things but then saw no reason why you should pay tax on a car at the same time.

"I remember asking him once if he ever paid income tax and he said 'Oh no sir, I wouldn't earn enough to pay income tax'. He had wads of money. 'I'll put it to you this way sir, if I'm out in the field or in the shed and I have a mare foaling, is there anyone from the tax office helping me to foal that mare? No, there isn't. So why should I have to give them any of my money?' Somehow, there was a bit of twisted logic in what he was saying. That was the way his mind worked."

Like all locals in Kilbeggan, the now-retired Garda was shocked and saddened by Mr Hanley's death.

"It upset people a lot, Christy was a well-known character and he was respected in the community. It was the first murder in the area since the early 70s, when an old lady about a mile outside the town was murdered for money. Kilbeggan is a very close-knit community, we'd have spates of burglaries for cash from time-to-time – burglaries when people would be out at bingo – but it's an area that's relatively crime free.

"Kilbeggan is basically one long street. The street starts at the Clara Road junction, then you go past the distillery, up what's known as The Hill, up Main Street, into The Square and out Upper Main Street. It's all old buildings, some three stories high. It was once a street that was home to lots of families but by the time I arrived there in the 90s, all the kids had grown up and no new families had come in, so it was a street of older people. Even now, it's been gradually depopulated and less and less people live on Main Street. Christy's was the first violent attack in decades in the area and because he was such a well-known character, it really hit everyone hard," said Mr O'Keefe.

Immediately following the crime, the response from the local community was brilliant. "The amount of information that people came forward with to help the Gardaí with the investigation was amazing. That was probably Cawley's downfall. A lot of people saw him and when the Gardaí got one piece of information that the two men had been spotted together, it all flowed from there. Everybody had their own suspicion about Cawley's involvement and the local people were brilliant when it came to helping with the investigation."

The killing of Christy Hanley came totally out of the blue.

"It was the last thing people expected to hear when they woke the next morning. He and Hannah were characters in the town. Christy was such an inoffensive man. I never once saw him lose his temper. He would always avoid a conflict and that's why it hurt people so much in the area."

Noel Cawley was sentenced in July 2009. He was jailed for 16 years for killing the pensioner and also received a concurrent 12-year sentence for stealing approximately €10,000 in cash from Mr Hanley's home. The judge backdated the sentence to June 24, 2008 – the date Cawley was taken into custody. He is due for release in June 2024.

Chapter 16
Mixed Emotions at Nally Verdict

There were mixed emotions outside the Four Courts in Dublin when news of Padraic Nally's acquittal began to circulate. Friends and supporters of the Mayo farmer hugged and shook each other's hands. There was a massive sense of relief that a little over one month before his 63rd birthday, Padraic Nally would be returning to his farm and to a life he had been unsure if he would ever see again.

In the hall outside the courtroom, phones rang and were quickly answered as the verdict of the jury was told and retold to friends and neighbours at home in Cross. Throughout the previous couple of weeks, villagers had been kept up-to-date with the happenings in Dublin and at last, the retrial had reached its conclusion. But while Nally's supporters were eager that the message would arrive home, there were no joyful celebrations among the crowd.

A wife had lost her husband, children had lost their father and nothing was going to change that or take from the heartache being felt by the Ward family.

Across the hall, the family and friends of John 'Frog' Ward were in turmoil. They hadn't thought for one second that the man who had shot and killed their loved one would be walking free from the Four Courts. The verdict in the Padraic Nally retrial sent shockwaves through the Travelling community and there were scenes of anger and anguish as the reality of the situation began to hit home.

Jimmy Ward, a brother of the deceased, was outraged at the verdict and claimed it is impossible for a Traveller to get a fair trial in Ireland. Jimmy admitted his brother had alcohol problems and had pulled a slash-hook on Gardaí on one occasion. Nonetheless, he argued there was no evidence that his brother had set out to rob Padraic Nally on the occasion of his death in October 2004.

Jimmy, who lives in Ballyshannon in Co Donegal, said 'every Traveller in Ireland' was upset about his brother's death. He added that his family felt it had been denied justice and that Travellers could not get a fair trial.

"If I go to a farmer's house today and knock on the front door and nobody answers and then I go to the back door and a man comes out with a gun and shoots me in the backyard, he'll say tomorrow I was there to rob the house and he'll get off," he remarked.

In Mayo, the local Traveller Support Group shared Mr Ward's opinion and said a Pandora's Box had been flung open by the 'not guilty' judgement, adding that difficult questions needed to be answered.

Continuing, the spokesperson said Travellers believed that the most obvious inference from the contentious verdict was that they are now regarded as having less value in Irish society due to their identity and ethnicity. Travellers, the spokesperson said, found it impossible to believe that a jury would have returned the same verdict if the victim had been settled.

"The Mayo Traveller Support Group believes the judgement will significantly undermine the belief of Travellers that they can get a fair trial in Ireland. It is difficult to see how a fair-minded jury could acquit Padraic Nally on the basis of the evidence that showed that John Ward was killed by a shot in the back as he departed Nally's farm, after he had been beaten 20 times by a wooden plank and after he had already been shot."

Not surprisingly, the Nally case sparked heated debate about the rights of individuals to protect their property and the Mayo Traveller Support Group expressed deep concern that the verdict would set a precedent and give the green light to individuals to take the law into their own hands.

They went on to point out that Travellers support their families by visiting homes to buy and sell a vast array of products and services and said there is a palpable fear that legitimately entering a property could now result in injury or death.

Rose Mary Maughan from the Mayo Traveller Support Group, gave her reaction to the judgement: "Travellers fear this will send out the message to society that it is perfectly alright to kill a Traveller. We don't feel protected by the law of the land. Personally, I feel my life is viewed as worthless by society. It is very frightening to think that someone can take the law into their own hands and kill someone."

Later that evening, across the road in O'Shea's Merchant, there was an unshakable conviction among Padraic's supporters that justice had prevailed.

During the difficult fortnight in the capital, Padraic's sister, friends, neighbours and supporters were amazed at how the people of Ireland reacted to Mr Nally on the streets of Dublin. Many shook his hand and wished him well, while a Wexford couple picked up the dinner tab one evening in O'Shea's.

Speaking after the verdict was announced, Padraic's friend and supporter Paddy Rock expressed his relief at the outcome.

"It's the result we've always hoped for and we're very pleased about the support that came for Padraic nationwide. Every single day, there were Mass Cards or letters or good wishes being sent, even through email, and Padraic was very thankful for it. We're glad it's over and we would like to just return to normal life – a life which was disturbed on Padraic Nally over two years ago, through no doing of his own," said Mr Rock.

Offering his deepest sympathy to the family of John Ward on behalf of the Padraic Nally Support Group, Mr Rock wished them the very best for the future. Continuing, he explained that the trial had taken a lot out of Padraic and explained that unfortunately, Mr Nally had to be taken into hospital during the trial.

"The stress was definitely the main part of it and it has taken a big toll on him, as it would with any normal human being. But I think, knowing the strength of Padraic, he can return to normal life. It will obviously take him quite a while but I think he can do it," opined Mr Rock.

Padraic's neighbour Michael Varley was also delighted when he heard the result and admitted he had been quite emotional when the jury announced their decision.

"Justice was done on the day. It's been a long time for Padraic's family, neighbours and friends. We're all relieved at this point in time that we can all get back to our own farms again and work in the community," he commented.

In a brief statement outside the court, Padraic thanked the jury members for their long deliberation and also his legal team of Brendan Grehan, Michael Bowman and Sean Foy. The farmer went on to thank his neighbours and friends, all of whom helped him along the way and all who sent letters to him.

"I feel sorry for the Ward family who have lost a father and are left with young children," he concluded.

Back in O'Shea's later, Padraic – who normally doesn't drink – settled his nerves with a brandy and said the verdict had been a big shock.

"I didn't think it would go my way but thank God it has. I was surprised at the outcome. I thought I'd be found guilty more than not guilty and I was prepared for prison, at least I'd been told I was anyway," he admitted.

Looking back on the fortnight in Dublin, the farmer said that it had been 'mighty stressful' and that he was 'all the time worrying and on edge'.

"It's a relief. To think that this night week I was going to hospital and tonight I've a verdict of not guilty from the courts," he added.

On Thursday December 7, 2006, Padraic spent a night in St James' Hospital, after getting severe chest pains.

"I was taken by ambulance from the hotel and put on oxygen. The doctors took blood samples and did some tests that night, then there were more tests on Friday and they put me on a walking machine to see about the state of my heart. I've been in a very stressed state since then, but I'm a bit more relaxed now," he confided.

Padraic was helped through the trial by his sister and the many friends and supporters who came along. It had meant a lot to the farmer to have so many of his neighbours and friends travelling the long distance to be with him during the retrial.

With the ordeal finally at an end, Padraic was looking forward to going back to his 30 cows and calves and was very appreciative that his friends looked after his farm and livestock in his absence.

Although he was looking forward to attempting to return to normality, he admitted he often thought about what happened on that fateful afternoon and stops to say a prayer for John Ward.

"It never goes away. I'm sorry for the Wards, they're without a father. And for the young children without a parent, it's a big loss."

When the verdict was announced, Padraic's only sister, Maureen, was naturally relieved and later that evening, she still couldn't describe what she felt in the courtroom.

"It's hard to describe, we've been through so much. It's hard to believe we're living in reality with all that's gone on. I think when the verdict was announced, we were grateful that the jury had been so thorough and careful. Today was very long and worrying and I thought it would never end. It's beginning to slightly sink in now but it's very hard to believe it," she confided.

Maureen also extended a word of thanks to all those who took the time to write to Padraic and to herself, to those who called to him, talked to him, sent Christmas Cards, Mass Cards, to the people who did all the work for him at home and supported him through the long and difficult period.

"It would have been very hard to carry on without all their help, all their encouragement, all their support," she said.

"I think it will take a few days or weeks to go back to normal but I would love if we could return to our normal lifestyle in the near future," she added.

* * *

The Padraic Nally case has been described as the most divisive case that Ireland has ever seen and the emotional debate unleashed by the not guilty verdict rages on, even now, a decade after the shooting. The immutable facts – regardless of personal opinions on the verdict – were that a father-of-11 was dead, a vulnerable farmer had to live with the guilt of killing another man, and life would never be the same again for the families and communities on either side of the debate. Whether people agreed or disagreed with the verdict of the jury, these facts were never going to change.

In the aftermath of the retrial, Traveller and settled communities once again found themselves pitted against each other in a no-win debate. All the old lines about a Traveller's life being less important than that of a settled person were trotted out by spokespeople for a group that never tires of telling society it is the most marginalised and most sinned against in the entire nation.

The Nally trial should never have become the catalyst for an emotive, divisive debate pitting Travellers against the settled community. Instead, it should have been the beginning of a better era for the elderly, vulnerable residents of rural Ireland.

The stark reality of the situation is that the case was nothing whatsoever to do with the rights of Travellers versus settled people and it was somewhat remarkable that members of the Traveller community were so keen to associate themselves with John Ward. Certainly, Mr Ward was a Traveller but, first and foremost, he was a dangerous criminal.

While many commentators at the time were not keen to get into the argument about the two communities, the reality of the situation is that if Traveller organisations want to win the confidence of settled communities, they need to start denouncing the likes of John Ward instead of finding excuses for unacceptable anti-social behaviour.

When John 'Frog' Ward arrived at Padraic Nally's farmyard in October 2004, he had already amassed a staggering list of 80 previous convictions in a crime-spree that began when he was still a teenager. His most recent performance involved threatening a Garda with a slash-hook.

While one never wants to speak ill of the dead, it would be utterly disingenuous to suggest that John Ward was anything other than a vicious – and possibly psychopathic – criminal. An autopsy on his body revealed he was ingesting a veritable cocktail of drugs – both legal and illegal – at the time of his death. He was not the sort of man one would want to walk past in the street, let alone confront in an isolated farmyard in rural South Mayo.

It didn't matter whether Ward was a Traveller or a member of the settled community; he was ultimately an inveterate criminal who turned his back on the norms of a civilised society and lived his life according to his own brutal dictum.

John Ward chose a life of crime. Padraic Nally did not. The farmer made split-second decisions when he was confronted with a criminal at his property in Funshinaugh, Cross, Co Mayo in October 2004. Throughout the legal proceedings following the death of Mr Ward, it was continually argued – both in court and in the media – that Mr Nally should not have reloaded his gun and shot John Ward in the back as he fled the scene. In truth, Padraic Nally made the life-altering decision in a state of panic. The situation he found himself in was not one he could have ever prepared for and it is difficult to imagine how any member of society would react if they found themselves in the same situation.

There were many suggestions after the retrial that the verdict would give rise to a 'licence to kill' policy in rural Ireland but that was little more than media hype. The loss of a life is always tragic and the outcome of the Nally case was not about to lead to normal citizens shooting the first criminal they encounter. The circumstances surrounding the shooting on Padraic Nally's farm in 2004 were out of the ordinary. Padraic Nally did not wake up that morning and go looking for trouble. Trouble came looking for him.

Chapter 17
Legislation to Protect Rights of Homeowners

In the wake of the verdict in the Padraic Nally retrial, Paddy Rock – one of the farmer's most loyal supporters – immediately called on the then Minister for Justice, Michael McDowell, to take a stand and introduce legislation to protect the rural residents of Mayo and Ireland.

The precarious legal position that existed in relation to the protection of a person's home, their family and their property, was at the forefront of people's minds. The preceding two years had taken its toll on Padraic Nally, his supporters and indeed the entire community in South Mayo. Since that fateful afternoon in the autumn of 2004, the people of Cross and the surrounding areas had become more and more concerned about their movements.

Outside Dublin's Four Courts, Mr Rock – spokesperson and leader of the Padraic Nally Support Group – said the decision by the jury to free the Mayo farmer offered Minister McDowell a platform to legislate for people in rural areas and for homeowners' rights.

"If the Minister trades off this platform and listens to what has happened, he shouldn't have any problem bringing in legislation to help people in rural Ireland," voiced Mr Rock.

Stressing that the case was never a 'Travellers versus settled people' issue, the Galway man opined that Minister McDowell should enact a homeowner's legislation so that people could be protected in their home and be in a position to defend their property.

"This is not a Traveller issue; it was coincidental that the person who arrived on Padraic Nally's land was a Traveller. This is an issue where an intruder came into a man's home. This is an issue where somebody crossed over a boundary. Minister McDowell should take note of this case, study it very carefully and legislate for the people of this country," added Mr Rock.

Continuing, he noted that, from the outset, the Nally Support Group had made it clear they had no animosity or axes to grind with the Travelling community.

"This was not and has never been a Traveller-bashing exercise, as some people in the media have reported. We extend our deepest sympathy to the Ward family and we wish them well for the future," he said.

Expressing relief at the outcome of the case, Mr Rock said the Minister for Justice had a duty to introduce law on the issue.

"This case has provided him with a platform to launch a Bill for the protection of people in their homes. He must ensure the Bill comes into play as soon as possible."

Nationally, it wasn't just Paddy Rock who was calling for new legislation. The dogs on the street could see there was a need to address the glaring anomaly created by the Nally verdict and pressure mounted on Minster McDowell to undertake the long-awaited reform of the law governing the rights of householders to repel intruders.

As the Nally and Ward families and friends attempted to pick up the pieces of their lives in the aftermath of the retrial, the focus of the public attention shifted to the issues that gave rise to the tragedy in Cross in October 2004. The consensus nationwide was that something would have to be done to ensure this sort of debacle would never be re-enacted in Irish society.

Of course, there were some legal and media commentators who suggested the verdict would be interpreted as a licence to kill and with this in mind, the necessary reform could not come quickly enough. A climate of fear had been created amongst elderly people in isolated communities all across the country and people needed to know the parameters within which they could operate when protecting their property and their lives. Unambiguous legislation – complex and all-encompassing – would be the only solution.

As one might expect – and despite calls from all sectors of society on the importance of immediacy in the introduction on new legislation – it was 2010 before there was any real indication of movement of the issue. That summer, the then Minister for Justice and Law Reform, Dermot Ahern, began the process for the introduction of new legislation.

In October 2010, Minister Ahern addressed his colleagues in Dáil Éireann in relation to the proposed Criminal Law (Defence and the Dwelling) Bill. He said the purpose of the Bill would be to clarify and restate the law on the use of force in defence of people and property in the context of an attack by an intruder in the family home.

The Bill, he noted, would ensure the law would be clear as to the rights of an occupier in defending themselves against a person entering their home with the intention of committing a crime. The Bill would also strive to strike the correct balance between the rights of the occupier and those of a trespasser.

Minister Ahern said he recognised and shared the 'very understandable public concern that exists with regard to attacks in the home' and described this kind of crime as intolerable.

"It strikes at the very heart of what most of us hold dear, that is, our homes and our loved ones."

Without specifically mentioning the Nally case, the Minister went on to point out that there had been a number of high profile and serious cases involving intruders entering homes with criminal intent.

"Fatalities have occurred and subsequent public comment has indicated the need for people to be certain of the legal position and to be reassured that there are laws in place to protect them," he said.

Continuing, he pointed out that the new Bill would address that need and allay any doubts on the issue which may be in people's minds.

"It is my intention to remove any ambiguity there may be in the law and to ensure that people are able to protect themselves, their property and others, in the home."

Quoting from the Non-Fatal Offences Against the Person Act 1997, the Minister stressed that the law had always provided that people could use force to protect themselves, to protect others and to protect their property.

"This Act sets out, among other matters, the rights of those who are required to exercise self-defence in the face of an attack. The Act permits the use of reasonable force in applying this kind of defence. The Bill I am bringing before the House deals specifically with matters relating to attacks in the dwelling and on the curtilage of the dwelling," he told the Dáil.

Minister Ahern said the people of Ireland are entitled to feel safe in their homes and to have the freedom to defend that safety if it is under threat.

"The home dwelling represents a sanctuary to us all which is generally regarded as more important than any other."

Minister Ahern went on to note that the Bill would ensure that people are aware that they may stand their ground in the face of an attack in the home; that there would be no exposure to civil liability if an intruder is injured as a result of force being used against him or her; and that the Bill acknowledges that the use of force may result in the death of an intruder.

In December 2011, the then Minister for Justice, Equality and Defence, Alan Shatter, moved to formally introduce new law to protect the rights of homeowners. Addressing Seanad Éireann on December 8 that year, the Minister said the legislation would bring clarity to the law on the use of force in defence of the dwelling and reflect the special status of the home in common law tradition and in the Constitution, striking the correct balance between the rights of the occupier and those of an intruder.

"People should feel safe in their homes. No one can disagree with that proposition. Our home is where we raise our children. It is where we spend time in the intimate company of family and friends. It is where we return at the end of the day to rest. It is where we live our private lives in peace, and it is our shelter from the world. An intrusion into the home is an intrusion into that shelter, that private life, that haven for the family. It is an attack on our peace of mind," he said.

The Minister explained that the Bill focused on the use of force by an occupier against an intruder entering the dwelling with criminal intent. The force used against the intruder, he said, must be reasonable in the circumstances the occupier believes themselves to be in, in order to protect himself or herself or others or property.

Minister Shatter acknowledged that the occupier may be mistaken as to the circumstances, but said that if their belief is honestly held, they would enjoy the protection of the Bill. Of course, the question as to whether the occupier's belief is honestly held would be a matter for a court or a jury to decide.

Continuing, he explained that the legislation would also clarify that it is immaterial whether the person using the force had a safe and practicable opportunity to retreat from the dwelling before using force.

In addition, the Bill would address the issue of injury and would not exclude the use of force causing death. This, the Minister said, was a carefully thought out provision and would not stand alone.

"It is in no way an encouragement or licence for unwarranted violence. It acknowledges the reality that a householder's aim should be to protect his home and family and that he is authorised to use reasonable force to do so."

He also noted that the Bill would provide that the lawful occupant would not be required to retreat from his or her dwelling when faced with an intruder and that a homeowner who uses 'reasonable and justifiable force' would not be liable in tort for any injury to the intruder arising from such force.

Concluding his address to the Seanad, Minister Shatter said the Act – once signed into law – would deal with some of the most fundamental rights of an individual: the right to life and the right to peaceful occupation of our homes. It would clarify the rights of householder and make it clear that unlawful intruders could rightly expect to face reasonable defensive force.

On December 9, 2011, the Bill passed all stages and was signed by President Michael D Higgins on December 19, 2011. Often referred to as the 'Padraic Nally Act', the Criminal Law (Defence and the Dwelling) Act 2011 came into effect on January 13, 2012.

Following the introduction of the long-awaited legislation, there were mixed reactions from legal and media commentators. The Irish Council for Civil Liberties spoke out against the Act, arguing that a law which encourages people to use lethal force to defend their property shows scant regard to the right to life of householders or intruders.

Of course, the Act does not actually encourage the use of force or provide homeowners with a licence to kill, but instead allows for reasonable force in certain circumstances. What is deemed 'reasonable' is subjective and depends on the individual circumstances. A person who uses force against an intruder, which results in the death of this person, still risks criminal prosecution if the force used is not deemed reasonable by the court or jury.

Whether the introduction of the Defence and the Dwelling Act would have made any difference if it was enacted prior to John Ward's arrival on the farmyard of Padraic Nally in October 2004 is questionable.

The Mayo farmer acted in the heat of the moment, believing his life and his property were in danger. Were a similar case to arise in Ireland today – taking into account the introduction in 2012 of the Defence and the Dwelling Act – the question as to whether or not the actions taken by the homeowner were justifiable would still remain a decision for the court or jury.

Chapter 18
Ward family: Picking up the Pieces

Winnie McDonagh was visiting family in Ballaghaderreen on the afternoon of Thursday, October 14, 2004. She had just sat down with a cup of coffee when her mobile phone sounded beside her. The caller informed her that a Traveller had been shot in an incident on a farm outside Cross in Co Mayo. The call ended and as she began to relay the information at the table, her phone rang for a second time. This time, the news was worse. Her brother, 42-year-old John Ward, was the man who had been shot in Mayo. Winnie couldn't believe her ears.

A short time later, another caller told her it had been a mistake and it wasn't John after all but when the phone rang again half-an-hour later, her worst fears were confirmed. Not only had her beloved brother been shot ... he had died as a result of his injuries.

Meanwhile in Tuam, Sally Sweeney – the youngest sister of John and Winnie – was going about her business at home when her mobile phone rang.

"I got a phone call to say that John was shot and I didn't believe it at first. I had been to see him in hospital a few days before that. I turned on the radio and the news was just breaking there too. All of a sudden, the phone started to ring and ring. Everyone wanted to know what had happened," she recalled.

Sally jumped in the car and drove to Cross but there were Gardaí on duty at the top of the road leading to Padraic Nally's house and she wasn't allowed any further.

"Some of the family were allowed down the lane and there was a tent in the field over John's body. I didn't go down that lane. I waited until they brought him to the hospital in Castlebar. Even still, I wouldn't go in to see him. He had got an awful death and I didn't want to see John like that," Sally continued.

John's family were understandably devastated when news of his death circulated.

"I could never get over what Padraic Nally did. When he shot him in the leg, he could have let him flee. I was back there shortly after John's death and I got a piece of flesh from the wall. I know it was wrong going into his house, totally wrong, but he didn't deserve to die," Winnie opined.

Winnie, who is five years younger than John, still maintains that her brother was at Nally's house to enquire about an old car or bits of scrap for sale.

"To me, he wasn't going in to rob him. He was in about the old cars. I'm not saying John was 100% perfect but Nally didn't have to kill him. If John was trying to rob him, he was totally wrong. John wasn't a saint, he had convictions and he used to do wrong things that he shouldn't have done, but there's no way he went into Nally's house to murder him or kill him. I faithfully believe he went in about the old car," she added.

Continuing, Winnie questioned why Padraic Nally didn't just shout at her brother and demand to know what John was doing on his property.

"When Nally saw John, he could have bet him and then called the guards. He shot him in the leg and then as he fled, he shot him in the back. Then he got his body and flung it over the wall like a head of cabbage. You wouldn't do that to an animal. Not in a lifetime would we do a thing like that. No member of the Travelling community would do a thing like that," Winnie said.

Winnie acknowledges that Padraic Nally was living in fear but claims he shouldn't have been allowed to walk free after killing her brother.

"He got away with murder. John was wrong to go into his place. Nally was an old man who lived alone and John shouldn't have gone into his property, but Nally shouldn't have come out after him onto the road and shot him. He took the law in his own hands. I know Nally said there had been things taken on him before but you don't take anyone's life into your own hands. He blew him to pieces. He should have let him flee. John wouldn't have got far and he couldn't have come back to hurt him," she reasoned.

It took a long time for it to sink in with John's family that the man they loved so dearly had been taken from them.

"He was laid out in Ballyshannon and to tell you the truth, it was a heartache. He got an awful cruel death and we'll never get over it," Sally explained.

"I keep talking about him at home, even to the children. I talk about Uncle John all the time and my baby is called John after him and after my father too. My oldest child, Katelynn, is 13 now. She was four at the time when he died," she said.

Neither Winnie nor Sally attended any of the court sittings after John's death.

"It was a waste of time at the end of it. Once the community got behind Nally, we weren't going to get anywhere. We knew once everybody took Nally's side, that was it. We all thought he'd be done for murder. He battered John with a stick, shot him in the leg and then shot him in the back," Winnie continued.

The 47-year-old believes that Padraic Nally will eventually pay for what he did.

"He only served 11 months in prison. He's still in fear and probably always will be but, in the line of John's family or any of our families, nobody will ever bother with him. We won't go near him or look for revenge. He'll pay for his crime at his judgement day," she added.

At the time of John's death, Winnie was living in Ballyhaunis.

"I used to listen to the radio and I got a lot of phone calls about what was in the paper. People used to keep the papers for me and give them to me but it got to a stage that I didn't want to look at it anymore. I needed to get away from it all so we moved away to Tralee but still, I couldn't get it out of my mind."

Eventually, Winnie decided to go and see a healing priest in Co Kerry.

"As soon as I went to see him, he could tell that I was very down and he knew that somebody had passed away belonging to me. I told him my brother was killed and that I was very hurt, I told him all about what had happened and he told me I had to let Padraic Nally go. He said to light seven candles for Nally and free him out of my mind. After a few weeks, I went into the chapel and lit the candles. I didn't think as much about him after that," she explained.

The priest also told Winnie to pray for John.

"I regularly light candles and get Masses said for John. He's never out of my mind. I used to have John's picture beside the television but I used to be focusing on that all the time instead of the telly. I have it in the sitting room now and I take it down and look at it all the time. He'll be with me always and I'll be thinking of him as long as I live," Winnie confided.

Not surprisingly, news of his son's death hit John Snr very hard. He had already buried his wife in January 1999 and he was heartbroken when his eldest son was laid to rest in Manorhamilton.

"It's unnatural to bury your child. He was in an awful state and he was always on about him, right up until his death at 73," Sally noted.

"He was really heartbroken over John's death and it put him on the drink for a while," Winnie added.

After John's funeral, the family began to see less and less of his wife, Marie. "She came for the first month's mind and the second month's mind and she couldn't get out of the chapel quick enough. She'd sit at her own end and she wouldn't spend time with us afterwards. That was in the first few months after he had died and we couldn't understand what was going on. I used to go up to see her in Galway. I wanted to keep up with her and I wanted to be there to comfort her if she needed any support, but every time I'd call to see her, she'd be gone off somewhere. Two or three of the children would be there and the kids would ring her and she'd say she'd be back in an hour but five hours later, she wouldn't be back. Once John died, she separated from our family," Winnie recalled.

Sally was having a similar experience with Marie. "I was ringing her to see if she was alright, asking if she needed anything done or needed the children watched. I often asked her to come and wait a weekend here with us in Tuam if she wanted but she was keeping her distance from us all," Sally explained.

Of course, there was another big shock on the horizon for the Ward family. In November 2006 – one month before Padraic Nally's retrial at Dublin's Four Courts – Marie Ward married 24-year-old Adam Abakker from Ghana. The pair tied the knot in a registry office in Longford and when news of the wedding appeared in the media a couple of days later, it was the first the Ward family knew of the union.

"It was worse than another death – God forgive me for saying that – but it was a big shock to us all to see her getting married so soon. John wasn't long dead and she was getting up and getting on with her life. It was a nightmare. We were just getting over John's death and then to hear that. To tell you the truth, I nearly had a massive heart attack. I nearly dropped dead." Sally said.

"I don't see any of John's children anymore. Charlie, his son, knocked on my door a few months ago and I had to look twice. I hadn't seen him in years. It'd be nice to keep in contact with them. Family is important and blood is thicker than water," Sally added.

* * *

On February 5, 2007, the family gathered once more in the Courthouse in Castlebar for the inquest into the death of John Ward. As expected, the inquest returned a narrative factual verdict, based on the evidence of the State Pathologist, Dr Marie Cassidy.

The inquest heard statements from a number of Gardaí, as well as from Padraic Nally and Tom Ward, among others. Garda Pauline Golden from Claremorris Garda Station read through her statement, which had been made at the time of the incident in Cross. It detailed the telephone call she had received from Padraic Nally after the shooting and her subsequent actions. Garda Peadar Brick from Headford Garda Station also read through his statement, which explained his involvement in the happenings of October 14, 2004.

The third statement to be read into court was that of Tom Ward, who had been with his father in Cross on that fateful afternoon. Tom's statement was read by Superintendent Padraic O'Toole and signed by Tom Ward. Sergeant James Carroll then read his statement, outlining his arrival at the scene and his ensuing interviews with Mr Nally.

Garda Stephen Clarke from Ballinrobe Garda Station read his statement to the court, based on the events of October 14. Michael Varley, a neighbour of Padraic Nally, had made a statement to the Gardaí following the incident and this was read by Superintendent Padraic O'Toole. Padraic Nally's statement was also read by the Superintendent and signed by Nally.

In his absence, the statement of Dr Michael Regan, who attended the scene that evening and pronounced John Ward dead, was read by the South Mayo Coroner, Mr John O'Dwyer. One of John Ward's brothers had also made a brief statement after formally identifying John's body and this statement was read to the court by Superintendent O'Toole.

Sergeant Eamon Breslin of the Divisional Scenes of Crime Unit in Castlebar was at the inquest to read through his own statement, detailing his arrival at the scene and his involvement in the case.

State Pathologist, Dr Marie Cassidy, had issued a 10-page statement following her examinations into the incident and at the inquest, she read through her conclusions. Dr Cassidy's evidence was detailed and extensive. It concluded that, following examinations, the State Pathologist found that Mr Ward's death was caused by the shotgun wounds to the trunk, with the blunt force trauma to the head a contributory factor.

When all of the statements had been heard, the South Mayo Coroner summarised the evidence for the jury of four men and two women. Mr O'Dwyer told the jury that they must decide on an appropriate verdict and pointed out that based on the two trials that had taken place, John Ward's death could not be described as 'accidental' or 'death by misadventure', nor could they decide to return an 'open verdict'. Furthermore, he warned that the jury could not go beyond the decision of the jury at the Central Criminal Court in Dublin.

Mr Dwyer suggested to the jury that they return what is known as a 'narrative verdict' – one that is simply a factual statement of what actually occurred. Accepting the Coroner's recommendation, Aidan Hope (foreman), on behalf of the jury, returned a verdict that John Ward, late of Carrowbrowne Halting Site, Headford Road, Galway, died as a result of a shotgun wound to the trunk, with the blunt force trauma to the head a contributory factor.

Mr Dwyer extended sympathy to Tom and Marie Ward and to the deceased's children, siblings, father and family. On behalf of the jury, Mr Hope extended sympathy to the Ward family and to Mr Nally and his sister Maureen. Superintendent Padraic O'Toole also offered the Gardaí's sympathy to the Ward family.

Speaking on behalf of both himself and Padraic Nally, Mr Nally's Solicitor Sean Foy extended sympathy to the Ward family and, acting on behalf of the Ward family, solicitor Paudge Dorrian thanked the various parties for their remarks. In addition, he paid tribute to the jury in the case and said that the matter could not have been finalised were it not for their verdict. Concluding, Mr Dorrian thanked Mr O'Dwyer for the manner in which he conducted the inquest.

* * *

In June 2011, there was heartache for the Ward family once more when John Snr passed away. He was laid to rest at the family burial ground in Manorhamilton. It didn't come as a surprise to the Ward family that Marie kept her distance that day. However, when John Paul Ward – a son of John and Marie – died in February 2013, she didn't turn up for the funeral either. In fact, only four of John Paul's siblings attended.

"A few of her children were there – Tom and two of the younger brothers and one of his sisters – four of them turned up at John Paul's funeral," Winnie explained.

John Paul was laid to rest in Manorhamilton, alongside his dad. The Ward family visit the grave as often as they can. "Anytime I go to Manorhamilton, I visit the grave and when we get together as a family, we chat about him. John was as good as a comedian. He could make his own jokes and make up songs. He'd make you laugh if you were crying. If you never had company and you had him, you'd be alright," Winnie remarked.

John's siblings will never forget their brother and they'll never forgive Padraic Nally for what he did. "I always think of him, no matter where I go. I never forget about him and I always hold his photo in the sitting room. I like to keep it there and keep him with me always," Winnie explained.

Although John was 18 and already married when Sally was born, she still has great memories of her brother and loves to hear her older siblings relaying tales from their youth. "We always talk about him when we meet up. The older ones would be telling the best of stories about him. John was a gas man, he was a character. There wasn't a bad bone in his body. Everyone has their ups and downs but he wasn't as bad as the papers put him down to be," Sally argued.

"That fellow, Nally, should have given him the chance. If he shot once, he should have shot in the air. There's a new law in now that if you enter someone's property, they have the right to shoot you. I think it's the worst thing they ever did. You'd be afraid now to enter anyone's property. What if you got a puncture outside? I'd be terrified for my life to knock on anybody's door. You can't just shoot someone for coming to your property. You have to give someone a chance to explain themselves. If John was given that chance, he'd still be with us today," she added.

Chapter 19
Tackling Crime in Rural Ireland

Padraic Nally's property had been targeted on several occasions prior to the incident on his farm in October 2004. A chainsaw had been taken, his bedroom had been turned upside down and, on more than one occasion, he had returned home to find somebody had been on his property while he was away. But despite his experiences – and those of his neighbours and friends – the Gardaí in Mayo were adamant that the area was by no means a crime hot-spot, certainly no more so than any other area in the county.

Retired Superintendent Padraic O'Toole, who headed up the investigation in 2004, said he wasn't aware of the Funshinaugh farmer prior to his arrival on the farm on October 14 that year.

"I had never come into contact with Padraic Nally before that. During the investigation, he spoke about burglaries in the area and the fear he had. Certainly, as the superintendent, I was aware of crime in South Mayo, but in that area – no more than the rest of Mayo and the western seaboard generally – crime figures would have been very low," he explained.

Nevertheless, the retired superintendent wasn't doubting that Mr Nally was living with a genuine fear.

"There's no denying that the fear of crime in the communities was very real and I've no doubt that Padraic Nally had a fear of crime and that fear was probably present elsewhere in the community too. The crime statistics wouldn't have suggested that the area was overrun with crime, any more than any other area of Mayo. In fact, the opposite was the case. The stats wouldn't have given us any cause for concern out there, but then, there are always crimes unfortunately and one crime is one too many," he admitted.

Mr O'Toole went on to note that it had transpired during the investigation that there were crimes that had allegedly been committed around the Cross area prior to October 2004 that weren't reported to the Gardaí. Of course, the retired superintendent – or indeed any serving member of An Garda Síochána – could not comment on the veracity of these alleged crimes.

"As Gardaí, we could only deal with crimes reported to us," he continued.

After the incident on his farm – and as Padraic Nally was awaiting trial for the murder of John Ward – he was visited on a number of occasions by members of the Gardaí.

"Clearly, we had to give crime prevention advice. Gardaí visited Padraic at home and talked to him about security. In any similar circumstances, the same thing would happen – regardless of who was involved – and Gardaí would have called to the house and given him advice about security and crime prevention," added Mr O'Toole.

At the time, there was much speculation about additional checkpoints and stronger Garda presence in the area but according to Padraic O'Toole, it was nothing out of the ordinary.

"There would have been Garda checkpoints in the area at the time. It was par for the course. We would have conducted checkpoints as part of the investigation process in an effort to talk to people who would regularly travel along that route in the hope of locating more witnesses," he explained.

Of course, the Gardaí were aware of additional movement and interest in the Cross area of South Mayo but they weren't unduly worried.

"There were no extra squad cars or extra patrols but clearly the Gardaí on duty would pay attention to the area whenever they were passing. From our point of view, we knew it was a curiosity point for people.

There were just ordinary people passing through the area that would swing by for a look. It was a kind of morbid curiosity really," he stated.

The retired superintendent realised there was a fear of retaliation from Padraic Nally's point of view.

"In all such cases, the Gardaí have to take that possibility into consideration. It would be remiss of us not to. Regardless of who was involved or what their background was, a member of a family had been shot and killed so we had a concern," he added.

Mr O'Toole would, however, debate the suggestion that there was an increase in fear in the area.

"There was definitely an increase in people talking about it but I don't believe the actual fear increased. Real or otherwise, that fear is there all the time. I'm from a country background myself and I'm aware of the concerns of elderly people living on their own. I've no doubt that fear is there and that it exists but, at the same time, there wasn't any increase in people contacting the Gardaí. There was an increase in awareness but I don't think that people started to expect that a house would be broken into every night as a result of this," he reasoned.

Interestingly, despite speculation at the time, there was no increase in gun licence applications in the region either.

"There are always new applications and renewals. At that time, gun licences were renewed annually, now it's every third year. Most people from a farming background have a gun anyway. There would be very little fluctuation in the number of gun licences from year-to-year," he explained.

* * *

Padraic O'Toole had only taken over as superintendent in the Claremorris Garda District in June 2004; four months prior to the shooting on the Nally farm. Of course, he would have loved to have had additional Garda resources at his disposal during his tenure in Claremorris, but the same could be said for any district in the country.

"You have what you have. There isn't a superintendent or a chief superintendent in the country who wouldn't take additional resources but it's important to point out that Garda resources weren't an issue in this incident," he stressed.

In recent years, there has been much debate about the closure of local Garda stations across rural Ireland but the retired superintendent admitted he doesn't have a problem with some of the closures.

"There's nothing wrong with a station closing when it's within a few miles of another station. In a time of stringent financial constraints, it's difficult to justify the need for all the smaller Garda stations. Some of the smaller stations – with only one or two Gardaí – are in close proximity to other larger stations and in many instances these stations are only four or five miles apart," he reasoned.

Despite the retired superintendent's reasonable logic, one of the by-products of the Padraic Nally trial was the emergence of a debate about the urgency of addressing rural policing in Ireland. In his evidence at the original murder trial in Castlebar, Padraic Nally revealed he had attempted to make contact with Gardaí in South Mayo on two occasions prior to October 14. He had called to his local Garda station in Ballinrobe to report thefts at his farm in Cross, only to discover that there was no Garda officer present on either occasion.

The crisis in rural policing had become progressively worse in the 20 years leading up to 2004, with Garda resources concentrated in the larger towns and many smaller stations operating on only a part-time basis in rural areas.

The Gardaí in the west of Ireland were doing their best in trying circumstances and it was by no means their fault that decisions had been taken at central government to close rural Garda stations. Gardaí could not be in two places at one time, particularly when the resources were already severely stretched in the larger towns.

The decrease in Garda resources had prompted many rural householders – especially the elderly – to come to the conclusion that they were on their own to fight against crime. The introduction of the Garda Reserve Force in 2006, by the then Justice Minister Michael McDowell, went some distance in allaying fears in rural Ireland and this volunteer reserve section of An Garda Síochána continues to be part and parcel of policing in every district across the country. Members of the Garda Reserve Force are paid an allowance and the personnel are of huge benefit and assistance to the Gardaí nationwide. Obviously, superintendents all over Ireland would prefer to have additional full-time Gardaí stationed in each area but in the absence of this, they welcomed the arrival of the part-time reserve members.

Karl Heller, superintendent with the National Crime Prevention Unit – in a message to the people of Ireland on the website of An Garda Síochána – says the Gardaí cannot fight crime alone, without the support and cooperation of the community.

"Everybody has a role to play in attempting to prevent and reduce crime. I would encourage all members of the community to actively consider how they can contribute to this goal," he continues.

Over the last number of years, in Garda districts all across the country – and in particular in rural Ireland – a concerted effort has been made by local officers to build relationships with communities and address the concerns of the people.

Joint Policing Committees (JPCs) have been introduced to develop greater consultation, cooperation and synergy on policing and crime issues between An Garda Síochána, local authorities and elected local representatives. JPCs also facilitate the participation of the community and voluntary sectors, with representatives from local organisations also sitting on these committees.

In addition, other initiatives have been undertaken across the country. In South Mayo for example, within the Claremorris Garda District – where Padraic Nally lives – local Superintendent Joe Doherty has made huge progress in smarter policing, rolling out local policing plans, communicating with residents on an ongoing basis and sharing the ownership of crime prevention with communities.

In each area within the district, Gardaí – in conjunction with the local residents – have compiled a list of names and numbers of people who can be contacted directly if and when there is any suspicious activity in an area.

In addition to this – and indeed the regular Neighbourhood Watch and Business Watch in towns and villages – Gardaí have established a Register of the Elderly for each area and these people are visited by members of the Gardaí on a regular basis, providing a friendly face and reassurance that the Gardaí are always at the other end of the phone.

The number one priority for Superintendent Doherty – and indeed for officers like him across the country – is to stamp out crime in rural Ireland. In this regard, the community alert system has become the cornerstone of rural policing nationwide, with communities working in partnership with local Gardaí through the structure of community alert.

The Text Alert System has also become an important tool for Gardaí, alerting members of the public to crime happening in their region and giving details of suspect vehicles or persons who may be involved in the commission of crime.

A partnership between An Garda Síochána, Muintir na Tíre, Neighbourhood Watch and the Irish Farmers' Association, the Text Alert system is an initiative being rolled out nationwide to facilitate immediate and cost-effective communication from An Garda Síochána to the public.

The system is operated in a structured and consistent way in conjunction with existing Community Crime Prevention Programmes (Community Alert, Neighbourhood Watch Group) and IFA branches. The Text Alert sees members of Gardaí providing information by text or email to each registered 'Community Contact'. They, in turn, forward the information by text or email to all members of their 'Community Group'.

At a meeting in the District Headquarters in late 2013, Superintendent Doherty sent out a clear message to the public; a message that echoes the views of every member of An Garda Síochána across Ireland.

"Community involvement is vital. The detection rate is improving all the time because people are reporting suspicious activity but we are still calling for more reports. If people see or hear anything out of the ordinary, the message is clear: lift the phone and call the Gardaí straight away. There's no point leaving it until the following day because the criminals will have moved on by then," he reasoned.

"Community alert is at the heart of policing all across rural Ireland. Through the Text Alert System and also through other initiatives introduced for smarter policing in rural Ireland – and with increased community involvement – we can all work together to stamp out crime," said Superintendent Doherty.

Chapter 20
Nally Returns to Life on the Farm

As a new week dawned on Monday, December 18, 2006, Padraic Nally was beginning to pick up the pieces of his life. He had returned to his farm in Cross in South Mayo and was continuing to come to terms with his dramatic acquittal for the manslaughter of John 'Frog' Ward.

The decision had prompted intense media and public debate throughout the country, with the case dominating the weekend newspapers.

Despite his relief at being back on his farm in Funshinaugh, Mr Nally remained fearful that he might become the victim of retaliation. The previous Saturday afternoon, he met with Sergeant Tony Cosgrove, the crime prevention officer with An Garda Síochána in Mayo, to discuss security arrangements.

"I didn't ask for any protection as such. Sergeant Cosgrove went through basic security with me and systems that should be put in place," Padraic explained.

Mr Nally admitted he was concerned that he might be targeted in an act of revenge.

"It's something I worry about a lot. When I'm on my own here, I don't know what time of the day or night there could be a retaliation. You have to just put your mind down to what you're doing, but you still have to be looking over your shoulder at all times."

Meanwhile, in the days that followed the acquittal, a spokesperson for An Garda Síochána said it was standard procedure for the Gardaí to hold a meeting with a person whose personal security might be in danger. The spokesperson noted that the Gardaí would be taking cognisance of the situation with Mr Nally but understandably, refused to disclose what action might be taken to counter any threat.

At 10am on that cold Monday morning, a heavy mist still lingered over the flooded fields of South Mayo. It was by no means ideal weather for farming but Padraic Nally was delighted to have his wellies on and be in a position to tend to his animals and his land. The quiet-spoken farmer said he had a huge amount of work to do on his 65-acre farm and was glad to be back amongst his neighbours, friends and animals.

Padraic never expected to be home for Christmas 2006. He was convinced he would be spending the festive season behind bars, as he had done the previous year.

"I'm delighted to be home. I didn't expect the verdict and I was prepared to return to prison. It's a great relief to know that it's all over. This time last year, I was facing Christmas knowing that I'd be spending it in prison and I had a lot of worries on my mind. Thankfully, I've no worries about going back into prison this year," he said.

Prison was a lonely spot for Padraic in 2005. "Christmas Day was just like any other ordinary day, except that there was turkey and ham for dinner. It was like any other day in prison, only lonelier, because I was away from home and missed being there and being with my family and friends. This year, it's a big relief to have my freedom back. I'll be here in Funshinaugh for Christmas and Maureen will be here as well. I'm looking forward to it but it's by no means a quiet time. Being on the farm, you have to look after a lot of things all the time, so it's hard to think about relaxing at this time of the year."

For the first 60 years of his life, Padraic Nally led a simple life. He went about his daily chores, called on neighbours from time-to-time, visited various marts across the region and attended Mass every weekend. That was the extent of his social calendar. Over the previous two years, the bachelor farmer had been catapulted into a media maelstrom. It was a life he wasn't prepared for but one he had learned to take on the chin.

"I suppose you have to accept that people want stories for the paper and radio and television stations. You have to just get on with it. I tend to look at the papers now and see the pictures of myself and see what has been written about me. In the last few days, I've just been reading the pieces surrounding my case and it is like the rest of the paper has no significance to me. Seeing myself on Prime Time and the News brought everything back to me about what happened here in October 2004 and as well, about the long fortnight that we spent in court in Dublin."

Of course, the stress of the retrial – as Padraic awaited his fate – had taken its toll on the farmer and he had been forced to spend a night in hospital during the trial.

"I'd say it was the stress. I was unwell all day on the Thursday in the court and I was sitting on a hard and firm bench, with no cushion under me or anything. My chest and my back were paining me quite a bit all day and when I went back to the hotel, I decided to go to my room. When I got up to the room, I was out of breath so I lay on the bed and fell asleep for a while. I got up again later and went down for a meal, but when I went down, I felt myself unwell again and I was saying to the neighbours that were with me that I was feeling unwell. They called the doctor and when he came, he ordered me to hospital," he recalled.

When the ambulance arrived that night, they took Padraic to St James' Hospital in Dublin.

"They put me on oxygen straight away going in on the ambulance and then on oxygen again when I got to the hospital. They kept me on it for about four hours and did various tests on me then and took blood samples. In the morning, I was put on a running machine and then they did more tests. It was Friday evening by the time they were happy to release me. Everybody was great in the hospital and I owe a big thank you to the ambulance staff, the doctor that attended to me in the hotel and the doctors and nurses in St James' who looked after me," he added.

Casting his mind back to his sentencing in November 2005, following the initial trial, Padraic said he was stunned at the court's decision to sentence him to six years in prison. Prior to this, he had never really spent any length of time away from Funshinaugh.

"It was a shock to me that I got so long for protecting my property and my home. Leaving Funshinaugh that day, it was hard knowing that I was facing a sentence and looking at being away from home for the first time. Before I left, I took a walk around the farm. I went out to the fields and sort of said goodbye to the animals," he recalled.

After being sentenced to six years in jail that Friday morning, Padraic was taken to Mountjoy, before being moved on Sunday morning to the Midlands Prison in Portlaoise.

Aside from the obvious position of not wanting to be locked up, Padraic was thankful to receive a favourable response on the inside. "A lot of the other prisoners came to me and identified themselves. They said I shouldn't be in there, when all I was trying to do was defend my house and my property. I got on well with everybody and I didn't interfere with anybody's business. The prison officers were good to me as well. I had different conversations with some of them at different times," he explained.

Two years on from the shooting and having been acquitted of all crimes, the Mayo farmer admitted he was still getting flashbacks from October 2004. "It has had a huge impact on my life. It's always there. All the time I recognise how lucky I was and how unfortunate the whole incident was. It was a tragic event in my life. I think about it all the time. My mind takes me through the events as they unfolded. It's like a picture in my mind all the time. I think about John Ward sometimes and I say a prayer for him."

As 2007 approached, most people would have expected Padraic Nally to be looking forward to the New Year but he was still somewhat apprehensive.

"I'm not looking forward to it as such. I'm at a low ebb at the present moment and it's hard to lift your life up all of a sudden at this time of year. The events in the last couple of years have been traumatic and it will take a while. I know the neighbours have been supportive in every way but they have their own lives to lead and have to go about their own daily work," he said.

Of course Padraic was – at the time – still not back to full health following his stay in hospital. "I'm on medication and I was told to take it easy from the hospital authorities, but I'm feeling alright besides. I'm worried about the state of my health so I'll be taking it a bit easier from now on. It will take a little while to really get back to normal. There has been so much heaped up on top of me in such a short time. I'm just looking forward to getting back to normal. In prison, there was no real exercise to keep you in a good physical state. You'd be sitting down for long hours and the work wasn't as heavy as that on the farm. It will take a while to get used to the climate again," he explained.

* * *

Eight years after his acquittal – and 10 years on from the death of John Ward – the events that led to and followed the shooting in Funshinaugh are still very much to the fore in Padraic Nally's mind.

"I had been tormented here at home for a couple of years leading up to October 2004. It had made me on edge and I was constantly watching cars and taking down number plates. A lot of burglaries had happened in the area at the time. It was mostly when people were out and they'd come home to find they had been broken into. The incident on October 14, 2004, is still very clear in my mind. It's all the time bothering me. Something like that never really leaves your mind, it's never really forgotten about," Padraic confided.

Even now, a decade on, Padraic is still contacted by people in various media organisations several times each year. At this stage, however, he has learned who he can and cannot trust. "I have to be careful who I talk to. Some people came here to the house to interview me and were rude. Some of them were trying to make a fool of me," he said.

Before the trial and retrial, Padraic Nally knew very little about the law and when he was advised not to take the stand in the retrial at the Four Courts, he wasn't sure what to think.

"It's awful hard to take advice when you know your own story. I had so much going through my mind but when it came to the retrial, my barrister told me it was best if I didn't go into the witness box. I knew he was giving me the best advice but I also felt I had a lot of stuff that needed to be told. There had been a lot of stories published about me that didn't help my case. People were saying stuff they shouldn't have been saying and I had a lot to tell in court. But at the same time, I was conscious my barrister knew what he was doing so I took that on board," he added.

While Padraic was delighted to return to his farm in December 2006 and was looking forward to returning to normality, it was a long time before he really settled in at home. "I thought I'd return to the old routine and to life as it was very quickly but it wasn't as easy as I thought. When I came home that December, I was still on edge. Maureen stayed in Funshinaugh for a while but she had to go home eventually. Really, it wasn't until the following May that I returned to any sort of normality. I was constantly fearful of attack," he recalled.

"I was warned not to be in the public eye too much but instead of that, there were cameras everywhere I looked. The guards came out to me and talked about security. They were worried there would be retaliation. For a while, there was a strong Garda presence around the place, day and night, and checkpoints on the road too. They monitored the area well," Padraic explained.

When he was initially released from prison in October 2006 and a retrial ordered, Padraic had some indication of what might lie ahead in the event of him being acquitted. "I wasn't sure what to expect or what might happen when I left Dublin on the day we won the appeal and I was freed until the retrial. I was being transported home and the sergeant at the Four Courts told me not to worry if anything happened along the journey. He told me that if there were any issues along the way, it would only take a matter of minutes before Dublin will be brought to a standstill. That gave me a bit of confidence. Coming down in the van, I was afraid we'd be stopped and I'd be attacked but the minibus had full contact with the Gardaí on the way home, making sure we weren't being followed."

Even when he reached home in December 2006 and was back in familiar territory, it wasn't a case of getting back to normal straight away. "The guards were calling around regularly and the doors had been changed and locks reinforced but I still didn't feel safe. The guards told me to call them if there was any trouble and I knew I could do that. I had a mobile phone at that stage but even so, I wasn't sleeping at night and it wasn't until the following May that I started to feel like I could begin to get back to normal. One day here in May 2007, I admitted to my sister Maureen that it was only then that I was getting back to normal and she said she was the same. She hadn't been sleeping properly either. We hadn't really discussed it up until then. Each of us were probably afraid we'd upset the other," he said.

While farming had been all that Padraic had ever known, he had made the decision before the retrial that if he was convicted, he was going to have to get rid of all his animals. "The neighbours had done more than enough while I was in prison. It was hard on them too. They kept everything going, as well as having to look after their own farms. I had come to the conclusion that things would have to change if I didn't get my appeal granted or if I had been sent to prison again following the retrial. I knew I would have had to make some difficult decisions then. I couldn't let them look after everything if I was going to be in prison for six years. I had it in my mind to get out of the animals," he said.

Padraic received thousands of letters and cards during his time in prison – so many, in fact, that they couldn't all be delivered to his cell. "The chief came to me one day and said there were a heap of letters. He was wondering if there was any way of getting them transported down home. He told me that the next time there was somebody coming to see me, to let him know and he could organise sending some bags of post home with them. There were over 3,000 letters and that was besides the ones that were delivered to the house in Funshinaugh."

One evening in early 2014, Padraic sat down to read some of the letters and cards he had received during his time in prison.

"I went through 2,000 of the letters one day – some I didn't even remember seeing before. Some were just being addressed to 'Padraic Nally, Farmer, Mayo' and they were still getting to me. I sat up late one night reading through more of the letters and cards and I was crying reading them. There was such compassion among the people writing to me," he confided.

Although Padraic faced his worst nightmare on his farm in October 2004 and lived to tell the tale, he remains concerned – both for himself and for people all over rural Ireland.

"It's not just old people being targeted. You're safe nowhere. People don't understand that. I was told I'd never get my gun back and I suppose I understand that but at the end of the day, a man has to defend his property when he's living in fear. I had to protect myself, my home and my property that day."

Despite claims, both in court and in the media, Padraic is adamant that he does not – nor has he ever had – anything against Travellers.

"I have nothing against the Traveller movement. They came to my house many times in the past for alms and they always got something and were satisfied. What happened in October 2004 was very different. John Ward was up to no good when he arrived on my farm. A few days after I shot him, he was due to appear in court in relation to a slash-hook incident with the guards. That's the sort of man he was," he said.

"People were making out that I had a grudge against Travellers and that's wrong. What happened on my farm – and what followed – had nothing whatsoever to do with Travellers. It was just me and another man. It didn't matter who he was. I felt I was under threat and in danger and I acted on the spur of the moment. A man lost his life that day and I'm sorry for the family of John Ward but I didn't get up that morning thinking I was going to kill someone. I'm not that sort of person. I didn't go looking for trouble. Trouble came looking for me."